Descartes' Meditations, Bro

A retelling of *Meditations on First Philosophy*

. . .

TOMMY MARANGES

Creator of *Philosophy Bro*

Printed in the United States of America
First Edition

Illustration by Jana Kinsman
Logotype by Adé Hogue

ISBN 978-0-692-56600-8

Philosophy Bro
1917 N Elston Ave
Chicago, IL 60642
bro@philosophybro.com

www.philosophybro.com

For my brilliant sisters
and my wonderful grandfather.

ACKNOWLEDGMENTS

. . .

As with almost any creative project by a solitary, misunderstood genius, *Descartes' Meditations, Bro* owes its existence to more than just a solitary, misunderstood genius. In fact, there probably wasn't a solitary, misunderstood genius involved at all. Sorry, I don't know why it occurred to me to even mention that.

I am super thankful for my creative team. My words-good editor Cory O'Brien was absolutely indispensable in making my words good; he was also brutally honest in all the ways I needed, especially telling me when I needed to do better and when to stop my fucking hand wringing. He's also just generally one of my favorite people. My philosophy editor Nathan Oseroff made sure that I was correctly interpreting Descartes' frequently ambiguous/poorly written arguments, and he did a hell of a job of it. The book is immeasurably better for his input. I ignored him at my own peril, and any disagreements you have with my interpretation should be brought to my attention, not his, because he'll just respond with "I tried to tell him." Chris Givens did the initial design work, and the images he contributed to the Kickstarter in particular made a huge difference. I'm *especially* grateful to my friend Brandon Keelean, who took over design and project management when the project fell behind schedule; he is an incredibly talented designer and an extremely generous friend, and I feel very lucky to have worked with him. I think I'm probably a nightmare to work for and he turned my shitty, haphazardly-formatted Word documents into the beautiful/useable thing you're holding. Thanks, team!

Thanks also to everyone who supported me in their own way while I worked on this book. Thanks to Cards Against Humanity and to Max Temkin in particular for letting me work out of their badass office and surrounding me with other very talented wonderful people. The book might never have existed without Max's very real support in so many tangible ways, especially his great advice on a staggering range of topics and his preternatural ability to know the right thing or person. Thanks to Katie DiPiero for her incredible patience with me in so many ways! Spending that much time with a philosophy writer who also thinks he's funny has to be just one fucking headache after another, but mostly she just kept me sane. I am super, super lucky for that. Thanks also to my family; my poor mother has had to tell all her friends that I'm "writing a book" and then listen to them talk about how their kids are getting promotions or MBAs or whatever bullshit. And you know what, she has never complained even once. I'm so glad I finished this book so that she could be vindicated in some small way. Also, the character in this book shits all over his father a whole bunch, but I promise, none of it reflects on my own relationship with my father.

Thanks to the philosophy department and the Glynn Family Honors Program at the University of Notre Dame, who couldn't have guessed they'd ever be dragged into something as low-brow as this, but here we are. Thanks in particular to the professors who put up with me begging my way into classes way above my weight class, especially Peter van Inwagen and Jim Sterba. I learned so, so much in those classes, and Philosophy Bro probably couldn't have existed without them, whatever mixed praise that counts for. Thanks most especially to Curtis Franks, who first taught me the *Meditations*, but also taught classes that changed the way I viewed the world completely and for the better. Curtis's classes taught me about being a philosopher, but amidst all my philosophy, also a human being.

Thanks to Kate, Rob, Troy, Steve, Ira, Chloe and everyone else I've worked with at the Princeton Review; I taught test prep to help pay the bills while I wrote, and they gave me a lot of great opportunities while covering my ass a whole bunch of times.

Okay holy shit, I can feel this turning into its own book. Uh, thanks to the community of speakers where the meaning of my swear-y, shitty argot resides? No, just a couple more now. Thanks to Nick Disabato for sharing his experience and lunches and for introducing me to Sheridan printing. Thanks to Nick Douglas for believing in me *very* early on and also for giving me my start as a paid writer. Thanks to everyone who read and commented on early drafts, but especially thanks to Arnav Dutt at Northwestern Law for pushing me on what I could accomplish in this book; it benefited greatly from his comments on an early draft, by which I mean he explained why my early draft sucked so bad and offered *several* very good suggestions that I'm glad I took.

Boy I hope I didn't leave anyone out, but what are the odds I got everyone? To anyone who deserved to be in these pages that I left out: you have to remember that I am super forgetful and also that I can be a tremendous asshole sometimes. I promise, I do regret your omission! Like, when I wrote this paragraph I was like "fuck I hope this doesn't actually apply to anyone," but I'm printing it just in case. Sorry.

Oh! Thanks to the Nerdologues, Bryan Duff, and especially Claire Friedman; they just fucking made my Kickstarter video for me, it's not like I offered to pay them or anything. Also thanks to Kickstarter for existing! I literally couldn't have done this without Kickstarter. Finally, thanks to everyone who backed the book and helped spread the word and generally made it so I could take a risk like this. I hope the book serves you, who brought it into the world, very well.

. . .

TOMMY MARANGES

NOTES ON TRANSLATION

. . .

Reproduced in this book is the *translation published by John Veight in 1901*, which has entered the public domain.

I also frequently consulted the remarkably clear Cottingham/Stoothoff/ Murdoch (typically referred to as CSM) translation of Descartes, published in *The Philosophical Writings of Descartes, Vol II* (1985). No portion of it is reproduced in my text, so if you're willing to drop some coin and you want the best *direct translation*, this is the one.

Descartes'
Meditations, Bro

INTRODUCTION

. . .

It's worth engaging with Descartes because he is a really, really frustrating writer, but there's just no way he wasn't a genius.

He's frustrating because, like so many really smart men, he's not happy being *really smart*; he also wants it to look effortless, like he just woke up with these great ideas. As you'll see if you glance at the original text (on the left throughout this book), there's this ridiculous narrative gloss over the whole thing where he's sitting at his desk in front of the fire, just scribbling this shit down as it comes to him, and then whoops! It just happens to be the work that helped found modern philosophy. It's fucking ridiculous. In reality, he worked really hard on this shit.

Because of the stupid casualism, first time readers are tempted to engage equally as casually. At least, I know I did that the first two times I encountered *Meditations on First Philosophy*. I was 18 and 20, so that didn't help, but both times, my classmates and I raised these terrible objections with just ludicrous amounts of confidence that we'd outmaneuvered one of the best minds of his time.

The thing is, with mercifully few exceptions, we tend not to teach books by idiots at the University level, and when we do they tend not to last as long as we've been teaching Descartes. Bertrand Russell called him the father of modern philosophy. Entire schools of thought have risen and fallen in the time since Russell, and we still teach Descartes. What are the *sheer odds* that we've all just *missed the thing* that will put an end to Descartes' legacy?

It turns out that *Meditations on First Philosophy*, for all its casual rhetorical pretense, is really several marvelously complex and technical pieces of philosophy, all interlocking. The conclusions are sometimes bizarre or too-confident, but the arguments are always careful and well-thought out. Descartes has thought of most of your objections already. Other great minds of his time objected early and often, and he published like *seven rounds* of replies to those objections. The point is that Descartes is smarter than he frequently gets credit for at the introductory level, but he's hardly bulletproof. Just, *underestimate him at your own risk.*

Despite the absurd premise and the thoroughly vulgar language, *Descartes' Meditations, Bro* is designed to be a genuinely useful tool for anyone who wants to understand exactly what the fuck Descartes is talking about. On the left-hand side, I've printed an English translation so you can compare the two and see what Descartes actually said. Sometimes Descartes packs a lot into a paragraph and I take a little longer to unpack it; sometimes he's showboating and I can do it in half the time. Either way, this produces large gaps on the page, which I've filled with lines for notes and annotation questions that emphasize keeping the larger project in view as you grapple with any given argument; understanding what the *machine* is supposed to do is frequently helpful for understanding what any given *piece* is doing.

In the spirit of "Descartes is a smart guy and a bad writer," I've made an effort to do as little argumentative work on his behalf as possible. In places where it isn't clear what he's saying, I've tried to rephrase him in a way that retains the ambiguity, but perhaps makes clearer what the options *are.* I worked almost entirely from the (translated) original, and I think this is a defensible and straight-forward retelling of the text; I'm aware that *Meditations* has been widely dissected and discussed, and that various interpretations get incredibly fine-grained or nitpicky. In a perfect world, those debates would be perfectly mappable onto my version, but, you know. You can't please all of the Descartes scholars all of the time.

I've learned a lot from doing this book, both about philosophy and about writing. I'm really grateful for the opportunity to do it, and I hope you find it helpful! If you have comments or questions, you can email me at *bro@philosophybro.com.* If you love the book or it saves your ass in a pinch and you want to buy me a drink, you can do so at *philosophybro.com/drink*. I try to keep an up-to-date record of what I'm drinking and a button where you can buy me one.

Thank you so much for your support, especially if you were a Kickstarter backer. This book couldn't have happened without you.

. . .

TOMMY MARANGES

MEDITATION I

. . .

Of The Things
Of Which We May Doubt.

01 —

SEVERAL years have now elapsed since I first became aware that I had accepted, even from my youth, many false opinions for true, and that consequently what I afterward based on such principles was highly doubtful; and from that time I was convinced of the necessity of undertaking once in my life to rid myself of all the opinions I had adopted, and of commencing anew the work of building from the foundation, if I desired to establish a firm and abiding superstructure in the sciences. But as this enterprise appeared to me to be one of great magnitude, I waited until I had attained an age so mature as to leave me no hope that at any stage of life more advanced I should be better able to execute my design. On this account, I have delayed so long that I should henceforth consider I was doing wrong were I still to consume in deliberation any of the time that now remains for action. To-day, then, since I have opportunely freed my mind from all cares [and am happily disturbed by no passions], and since I am in the secure possession of leisure in a peaceable retirement, I will at length apply myself earnestly and freely to the general overthrow of all my former opinions.

MEDITATION I

. . .

Of The Things
Of Which We May Doubt.

— **01**

HOLY SHIT FUCK ME, it feels like my eyeballs are going to explode. I barely remember shit, I lost my phone, I blew the entire Spring Break budget in one night and all I have to show for it is this fucking terrible hangover. Goddammit I hope I had a good time last night.

This isn't my fault. I thought that dude was my personal hero, world's greatest lacrosse player Paul Rabil. Anyone would have done what I did in that position: assumed he'd pay for all those drinks. I thought he was the highest-paid lacrosse player in the world. That's how beliefs work: you believe some shit to begin with and then build other beliefs on top of that. If you don't start out with a firm foundation, the whole structure is going to be just a disaster of half-truths and bad guesses. My mistake wasn't partying too hard, my mistake was partying for the wrong reasons.

Ugh, here's a terrible thought: what if I'm wrong about other shit, too? Like, what if I'm wrong about something even more important than Spring Break? That would be catastrophic. I built the foundations of my beliefs when I was, what, a kid? Some idiot youth? If I'm stuck on this gorgeous beach all day nursing a hangover like an asshole, I might as well tear down my beliefs, start totally from scratch so I never make a mistake like this again.

But, to this end, it will not be necessary for me to show that the whole of these are false—a point, perhaps, which I shall never reach; but as even now my reason convinces me that I ought not the less carefully to withhold belief from what is not entirely certain and indubitable, than from what is manifestly false, it will be sufficient to justify the rejection of the whole if I shall find in each some ground for doubt. Nor for this purpose will it be necessary even to deal with each belief individually, which would be truly an endless labor; but, as the removal from below of the foundation necessarily involves the downfall of the whole edifice, I will at once approach the criticism of the principles on which all my former beliefs rested.

All that I have, up to this moment, accepted as possessed of the highest truth and certainty, I received either from or through the senses. I observed, however, that these sometimes misled us; and it is the part of prudence not to place absolute confidence in that by which we have even once been deceived.

WHAT IS OUR HERO'S GOAL FOR THIS PROJECT?

But it may be said, perhaps, that, although the senses occasionally mislead us respecting minute objects, and such as are so far removed from us as to be beyond the reach of close observation, there are yet many other of their informations (presentations), of the truth of which it is manifestly impossible to doubt; as for example, that I am in this place, seated by the fire, clothed in a winter dressing gown, that

— 02

This time I'll make sure I have a firm, solid foundation for my beliefs; once I'm sure I have no false beliefs, I can build safely upward. Plus, if I do that, I don't have to go through and check each belief individually. I don't have time to check all my very specific beliefs about lowland scotch and which clubs belong in my golf bag and why squats are my real dad; way easier to just start fresh. This time, I'm only going to believe something if I can be *absolutely certain* that it's true. If I can't be sure of something, like if there's any room to doubt it at all, then I'm going to just absolutely refuse to accept it, like it's a comment on my lifestyle from some fucking casual.

— 03

I guess the first thing at the foundations of my beliefs is my trust in my senses? That's how last night's ordeal got started: my senses were like, "Yeah dude that's definitely Paul Rabil over there." I was all, "Hell yeah, Paul Rabil is the man and I am totally going to party with him." Fuck me for thinking that just because someone looks *exactly like Paul Rabil* in poor lighting conditions, he really is Paul Rabil, right? Obviously since my senses can be so wrong about something so important, I can't trust them at all. Trick me into thinking some rando is Paul Rabil once, shame on you, senses. Trick me into thinking some rando is Paul Rabil twice, shame on me for trusting my senses again.

— 04

Maybe my senses are like, "Aw, dude, c'mon. Really?" Yes, senses, fuck you. "You can't trust us at all?" Nope. "Look, we're sorry we fucked up the Paul Rabil thing. The lighting was terrible, and we didn't think anyone else would have a crispy flow like that. But you can still trust us on the big things, the really obvious stuff, right? Like, you're definitely sitting on a beach getting an incredible tan. That's definitely a beach in front

I hold in my hands this piece of paper, with other intimations of the same nature. But how could I deny that I possess these hands and this body, and withal escape being classed with persons in a state of insanity, whose brains are so disordered and clouded by dark bilious vapors as to cause them pertinaciously to assert that they are monarchs when they are in the greatest poverty; or clothed [in gold] and purple when destitute of any covering; or that their head is made of clay, their body of glass, or that they are gourds? I should certainly be not less insane than they, were I to regulate my procedure according to examples so extravagant.

05 —

Though this be true, I must nevertheless here consider that I am a man, and that, consequently, I am in the habit of sleeping, and representing to myself in dreams those same things, or even sometimes others less probable, which the insane think are presented to them in their waking moments. How often have I dreamt that I was in these familiar circumstances, that I was dressed, and occupied this place by the fire, when I was lying undressed in bed? At the present moment, however, I certainly look upon this paper with eyes wide awake; the head which I now move is not asleep; I extend this hand consciously and with express purpose, and I perceive it; the occurrences in sleep are not so distinct as all this. But I cannot forget that, at other times I have been deceived in sleep by similar illusions; and, attentively considering those cases, I perceive so clearly that there exist no certain marks by which the state of waking can ever be distinguished from sleep, that I feel greatly astonished; and in amazement I almost persuade myself that I am now dreaming.

06 —

Let us suppose, then, that we are dreaming, and that all these particulars—namely, the opening of the eyes, the motion of the head,

of you, and you definitely have a tan handsome body that all your haters are jealous of. There's *no way* we could fuck up *that* badly. Maybe we don't get everything right all the time, but just because we fuck up sometimes in dimly lit bars or when shit is very far away doesn't mean you should doubt *literally everything*. You would have to be a crazy person to doubt *everything*. That's like thinking you're actually made of bronze or that your face is a jello shot or that you shouldn't go out drinking again tonight."

— **05**

But no, still fuck you, senses, even about shit like "I have a body." That seems obvious now, but what if I'm dreaming or some shit? Sometimes I really do dream crazy shit like "My face is not a face, it is instead a paper cup filled with jello and vodka" and it seems totally normal while I'm in the dream. Sometimes I also dream boring shit like "I'm just sitting on the beach hanging out and tanning" when I'm actually passed out on a couch or the floor or dangling over a third floor balcony, snoring and drooling and not tanning at all. This doesn't seem fuzzy and hazy like a dream; it seems like I am in complete control, like I can bring this beer to my lips whenever I want. But that's exactly what a dreaming bro *would* say. It *seems* like I'm awake and alert, but it always seems like that, even when my dreams are as crazy as "Oh no, guys, my face is definitely an apple-flavored gelatinous shot made with fermented potato juice, but at least my dad is here for me."

— **06**

Since I could be dreaming right now, I have to act like everything my senses tell me is bogus. This beach, the blue sky, all those people over there,

the forth-putting of the hands—are merely illusions; and even that we really possess neither an entire body nor hands such as we see. Nevertheless it must be admitted at least that the objects which appear to us in sleep are, as it were, painted representations which could not have been formed unless in the likeness of realities; and, therefore, that those general objects, at all events, namely, eyes, a head, hands, and an entire body, are not simply imaginary, but really existent. For, in truth, painters themselves, even when they study to represent sirens and satyrs by forms the most fantastic and extraordinary, cannot bestow upon them natures absolutely new, but can only make a certain medley of the members of different animals; or if they chance to imagine something so novel that nothing at all similar has ever been seen before, and such as is, therefore, purely fictitious and absolutely false, it is at least certain that the colors of which this is composed are real. And on the same principle, although these general objects, *viz.* [a body], eyes, a head, hands, and the like, be imaginary, we are nevertheless absolutely necessitated to admit the reality at least of some other objects still more simple and universal than these, of which, just as of certain real colors, all those images of things, whether true and real, or false and fantastic, that are found in our consciousness (*cogitatio*), are formed.

07 —

To this class of objects seem to belong corporeal nature in general and its extension; the figure of extended things, their quantity or magnitude, and their number, as also the place in, and the time during, which they exist, and other things of the same sort.

even the fact that I have a body: I have to assume all of that shit is just a dream. Wouldn't it be nice if this was all a dream, and I didn't actually blow all that money on fucking bottle service for some Paul-Rabil-looking-ass motherfucker? Hope I wake up soon! Ugh, what's left? Am I even allowed to believe in money? Yeah, I guess so. Even if I'm dreaming right now, there's still a bunch of shit I could believe in, like the general ideas of the things I'm dreaming about. The *general ideas* in a dream have to come from somewhere. Even my crazy jello-faced nightmares have some basis in reality: jello shots and faces are real things in the world, or else I couldn't even dream about them. Or even if I'm totally making up faces and jello shots, I'm making it up out of *something*. I couldn't have *totally invented* every single thing about bodies; if I'm dreaming, there have to be some basic things that these dream-bodies are *built out of*.

WHY ISN'T THE "I'M DREAMING" SCENARIO SKEPTICAL ENOUGH FOR OUR HERO?

— **07**

Like maybe right now I'm dreaming that I have a body that takes up space and has a really handsome shape, and that there are like five other people on the beach this morning, and that holy fuck ME am I hungover. Even if that's all just a dream and absolutely no bodies *actually* exist, I can still believe that taking up space and having a shape and being in a place at a time is all the sort of shit that bodies *would do*.

We will not, therefore, perhaps reason illegitimately if we conclude from this that Physics, Astronomy, Medicine, and all the other sciences that have for their end the consideration of composite objects, are indeed of a doubtful character; but that Arithmetic, Geometry, and the other sciences of the same class, which regard merely the simplest and most general objects, and scarcely inquire whether or not these are really existent, contain somewhat that is certain and indubitable: for whether I am awake or dreaming, it remains true that two and three make five, and that a square has but four sides; nor does it seem possible that truths so apparent can ever fall under a suspicion of falsity [or incertitude].

Nevertheless, the belief that there is a God who is all powerful, and who created me, such as I am, has, for a long time, obtained steady possession of my mind. How, then, do I know that he has not arranged that there should be neither earth, nor sky, nor any extended thing, nor figure, nor magnitude, nor place, providing at the same time, however, for [the rise in me of the perceptions of all these objects, and] the persuasion that these do not exist otherwise than as I perceive them? And further, as I sometimes think that others are in error respecting matters of which they believe themselves to possess a perfect knowledge, how do I know that I am not also deceived each time I add together two and three, or number the sides of a square, or form some judgment still more simple, if more simple indeed can be imagined? But perhaps Deity has not been willing that I should be thus deceived, for he is said to be supremely good. If, however, it were repugnant to

— 08

Since I don't know about specific bodies, I have to doubt, like, physics (I've definitely dreamed crazier physics than this before) and biology (since butts could be way different) and chemistry (since there might be different, weird chemicals that cause hangovers, I don't fucking know). Really I just have to doubt everything I ever learned in that weird-smelling science building. But I don't have to doubt math at all. Like maybe the whole physical world is just a dream, but math doesn't give a fuck whether anything physical actually exists or not. Math isn't saying there *really are* three dudes and two ladies over there; it's just saying that would be a total of five people, whether or not they're real. It's like, "I'm Geometry, and I don't give a fuck about whether you actually have a triangle for a dick. All I know is, dream or no dream, a triangle dick has three sides and the angles add up to 180 degrees. Geometry out!" and then Geometry drops the mic and I'm like, "Damn, Geometry, have you been working out? How am I supposed to doubt you?"

— 09

NO WAIT STOP HERE'S HOW. Maybe this is stupid, but what if there's an all-powerful God? I don't know there *isn't* one, and if He does exist, He could fuck with me however He wanted. He could make me think of beaches and bodies and shapes and numbers, all the shit I'm possibly dreaming about right now, even if none of that shit existed at all.

Even without an all-powerful Douchebag lying to me, I've definitely fucked up pretty simple math before by not paying attention. "$100 plus a 20% tip is $20, so that's $300, right? No, wait, fuck me." God could absolutely fuck with me every time I try to do addition; maybe 2+3=8, and I've just never noticed. I *can't* notice, God won't let me. Maybe triangles have four sides and God is hiding one. I grew up learning that God is loving and kind and a good kisser or whatever, but what kind of loving God would allow RabilGate? If He lets me get lied to *sometimes*, how do I know I'm not getting lied to *constantly*?

the goodness of Deity to have created me subject to constant deception, it would seem likewise to be contrary to his goodness to allow me to be occasionally deceived; and yet it is clear that this is permitted.

10 —

Some, indeed, might perhaps be found who would be disposed rather to deny the existence of a Being so powerful than to believe that there is nothing certain. But let us for the present refrain from opposing this opinion, and grant that all which is here said of a Deity is fabulous: nevertheless, in whatever way it be supposed that I reach the state in which I exist, whether by fate, or chance, or by an endless series of antecedents and consequents, or by any other means, it is clear (since to be deceived and to err is a certain defect) that the probability of my being so imperfect as to be the constant victim of deception, will be increased exactly in proportion as the power possessed by the cause, to which they assign my origin, is lessened. To these reasonings I have assuredly nothing to reply, but am constrained at last to avow that there is nothing of all that I formerly believed to be true of which it is impossible to doubt, and that not through thoughtlessness or levity, but from cogent and maturely considered reasons; so that henceforward, if I desire to discover anything certain, I ought not the less carefully to refrain from assenting to those same opinions than to what might be shown to be manifestly false.

11 —

But it is not sufficient to have made these observations; care must be taken likewise to keep them in remembrance. For those old and customary opinions perpetually recur—long and familiar usage giving them the right of occupying my mind, even almost against my will, and subduing my belief; nor will I lose the habit of deferring to them and confiding in them so long as I shall consider them to be what in

— **10**

Woah, wait a second, God can't bend the very rules of *logic*, can He? Like, He's powerful, but is He so powerful He can make circles with corners or a bad Dave Matthews Band album? Well, if God isn't powerful enough to bend logic, we're now dealing with a less-powerful God. Maybe I was made by some asshole freshman God in Pottery 101, but then if that's true He probably fucked up making me. If I'm a shitty creation, then I'll probably fuck up math anyway without God's help. The more powerful God is, the more shit He can lie to me about; the less powerful God is, the more shit I'll fuck up on my own without needing to be lied to. Either way, I can't be absolutely sure in my beliefs about math, so I have to doubt it.

HOW IS "GOD MIGHT BE A DICK" A MORE USEFUL SCENARIO THAN "I'M DREAMING?"

— **11**

How the fuck am I going to *doubt math*? I'm too hungover for this shit, I'm exhausted. How bad could it be to just assume I have a body, right? That seems really obvious! And surely I can trust my senses for *some* things, right? And, oh, *maybe* sometimes my senses are weird, but *surely* I would recognize my idol Paul Rabil, right? And just like that, I'm back in the same shitty position. It's *so easy* to just start believing shit until it's

truth they are, viz, opinions to some extent doubtful, as I have already shown, but still highly probable, and such as it is much more reasonable to believe than deny. It is for this reason I am persuaded that I shall not be doing wrong, if, taking an opposite judgment of deliberate design, I become my own deceiver, by supposing, for a time, that all those opinions are entirely false and imaginary, until at length, having thus balanced my old by my new prejudices, my judgment shall no longer be turned aside by perverted usage from the path that may conduct to the perception of truth. For I am assured that, meanwhile, there will arise neither peril nor error from this course, and that I cannot for the present yield too much to distrust, since the end I now seek is not action but knowledge.

12 —

I will suppose, then, not that Deity, who is sovereignly good and the fountain of truth, but that some malignant demon, who is at once exceedingly potent and deceitful, has employed all his artifice to deceive me; I will suppose that the sky, the air, the earth, colors, figures, sounds, and all external things, are nothing better than the illusions of dreams, by means of which this being has laid snares for my credulity; I will consider myself as without hands, eyes, flesh, blood, or any of the senses, and as falsely believing that I am possessed of these; I will continue resolutely fixed in this belief, and if indeed by this means it be not in my power to arrive at the knowledge of truth, I shall at least do what is in my power, *viz.*, [suspend my judgment], and guard with settled purpose against giving my assent to what is false, and being imposed upon by this deceiver, whatever be his power and artifice. But this undertaking is arduous, and a certain indolence insensibly leads me back to my ordinary course of life; and just as the captive, who, perchance, was enjoying in his dreams an imaginary liberty, when he begins to suspect that it is but a vision, dreads awakening, and conspires with the agreeable illusions that the deception may be

too late and you fuck up. It's an easy start at "I have a body," but it's such a slippery slope from there.

So instead of staying neutral I'll just go real hard in the other direction: I'll actively convince myself that things are probably false. As long as I can come up with *some argument* against believing something, I'll be able to doubt it; the argument doesn't have to be *good*, it just has to be *an argument*. So maybe I'll be like, "I want to trust my senses but what if, fuck, I don't know, what if a dog is in charge of everything?" If I'm going to trust my senses, I need to be able to overcome shit even as simple as "What if it's a dog?" It's a bad argument, but it's also like a bookmark for my doubts so I don't start just believing in butts and spotting lacrosse god Paul Rabil everywhere.

— **12**

Or maybe it's not a dog running *everything*. Maybe there's an evil demon actively fucking with me, just trying his best to make sure I don't learn anything. He's made me believe in all this shit like days at the beach and blue skies and my best bros and sick jams, and what if it turns out that none of that shit was real? What if I spent all that time in the gym and getting a tan and standing in front of a mirror and it turns out my body doesn't actually exist at all? What if it's all an illusion, right down to the eyes I use to take it all in? I don't know about *anything* for certain, but if I want to keep this demon from fooling me any longer, I have to assume that *all of it* is an illusion after all. I have to doubt everything, which, fuck, that is so heavy. This week was supposed to be a vacation, and instead it feels like I'm being thrown into some insane house ritual where I can't breathe and up is down and nothing makes sense.

You know what, fuck this. I had a terrible night last night and an even weirder day and right now, I don't actually give a shit whether an evil demon is fooling me or not. I just want my life back for a night. So here's the plan: I'mma get fucked up and have a good-ass time. If it's an illusion, fuck it, I'm going to enjoy it anyway for as long as I can.

prolonged; so I, of my own accord, fall back into the train of my former beliefs, and fear to arouse myself from my slumber, lest the time of laborious wakefulness that would succeed this quiet rest, in place of bringing any light of day, should prove inadequate to dispel the darkness that will arise from the difficulties that have now been raised.

OUR HERO DOESN'T REALLY BELIEVE IN AN EVIL DEMON, SO WHY DOES
HE ADOPT THAT BELIEF TEMPORARILY?

MEDITATION II

. . .

Of The Nature of The Human Mind; And That It Is More Easily Known Than The Body.

01 —

The Meditation of yesterday has filled my mind with so many doubts, that it is no longer in my power to forget them. Nor do I see, meanwhile, any principle on which they can be resolved; and, just as if I had fallen all of a sudden into very deep water, I am so greatly disconcerted as to be unable either to plant my feet firmly on the bottom or sustain myself by swimming on the surface. I will, nevertheless, make an effort, and try anew the same path on which I had entered yesterday, that is, proceed by casting aside all that admits of the slightest doubt, not less than if I had discovered it to be absolutely false; and I will continue always in this track until I shall find something that is certain, or at least, if I can do nothing more, until I shall know with certainty that there is nothing certain. Archimedes, that he might transport the entire globe from the place it occupied to another, demanded only a point that was firm and immovable; so, also, I shall be entitled to entertain the highest expectations, if I am fortunate enough to discover only one thing that is certain and indubitable.

02 —

I suppose, accordingly, that all the things which I see are false (fictitious); I believe that none of those objects which my fallacious memo-

MEDITATION II

. . .

Of The Nature of The Human Mind;
And That It Is More Easily Known Than The Body.

— **01**

Aw, fuck me. I tried real hard to drink away yesterday's *insane* self-doubts, but it didn't work. Now either I have this awful fucking hangover, or I don't have a body to *be* hungover and the demon is punishing me for trying to escape this despair. I have to try to sort out which one it is, and as far as I can tell the best way to do that is to take everything I ever thought I knew, throw that shit out the window, and start completely from scratch. Okay, done, but now I have no idea where to go next. Is there even one single thing I can be sure of, one thing I can grab onto to keep from losing my mind?

WHAT IS THE GOAL FOR THIS MEDITATION? HOW DOES IT RELATE TO THE LAST MEDITATION?

— **02**

Well, there sure is a lot of shit I *can't* be sure of yet; like, I definitely have to assume that my sight is totally unreliable. It *seems* like I'm drinking

ry represents ever existed; I suppose that I possess no senses; I believe that body, figure, extension, motion, and place are merely fictions of my mind. What is there, then, that can be esteemed true? Perhaps this only, that there is absolutely nothing certain.

WHY DOESN'T OUR HERO JUST PACK IT UP AND GO HOME AFTER HE PROVES HIS OWN EXISTENCE?

03 —

But how do I know that there is not something different altogether from the objects I have now enumerated, of which it is impossible to entertain the slightest doubt? Is there not a God, or some being, by whatever name I may designate him, who causes these thoughts to arise in my mind? But why suppose such a being, for it may be I my-self am capable of producing them? Am I, then, at least not something? But I before denied that I possessed senses or a body; I hesitate, how-ever, for what follows from that? Am I so dependent on the body and the senses that without these I cannot exist? But I had the persuasion that there was absolutely nothing in the world, that there was no sky and no earth, neither minds nor bodies; was I not, therefore, at the same time, persuaded that I did not exist? Far from it; I assuredly existed, since I was persuaded. But there is I know not what being, who is possessed at once of the highest power and the deepest cunning, who is constantly employing all his ingenuity in deceiving me. Doubt-less, then, I exist, since I am deceived; and, let him deceive me as he may, he can never bring it about that I am nothing, so long as I shall be conscious that I am something. So that it must, in fine, be maintained,

on a beach, but since my sight fucks shit up a bunch, I don't know if this beach or these people or this cool, nurturing beer are even real. And since my memory also fucks up sometimes, everything in my memory has to go, too. Just the other day I was like, "Hey, Chad is coming to this party, right?" And my bros were like, "Dude. Chad is dead, remember?"

Oh, fuck, that's right. That crazy weekend? The investigation? Those endless hearings? Those are just memories now. It's all just memories now, there's nothing left but memories. I saw his body, I saw where it ended up, but I don't even know if bodies or their shapes or movement through the air or places to land even exist, I just don't know. That memory is so vivid when it comes back, but I totally forgot until just now. Fuck me completely.

— **03**

This is so much worse than I thought. My senses, my memories, even internet weightlifting forums—I can't trust any of it. There has to be something, maybe something that isn't physical at all. Maybe God! Maybe, maybe there's a God after all and He's the one putting these thoughts in my head. But no, even then, I could just be making these thoughts up myself. Maybe I really have nothing to hold on to.

Well, wait. Who is it that has nothing? Like, if all that shit is an illusion, and I'm not real, *who's* being fooled? Even if this is just some incredibly complicated prank, even if the prank is on the *cosmic fucking level*, like some really, seriously powerful anti-God is doing this to me, no matter how fucking awful it is, don't I have to exist to *be* pranked? Otherwise, there's no one to be pranked. When I ask "Do I even exist?" the question kind of answers itself: I have to exist first to ask it. So as long as I'm doubting or perceiving or thinking about butts or beer or really anything at all, I have at least one thing I can be sure of: *I exist*.

all things being maturely and carefully considered, that this propo-
sition (*pronunciatum*) I am, I exist, is necessarily true each time it is
expressed by me, or conceived in my mind.

04 —

But I do not yet know with sufficient clearness what I am, though
assured that I am; and hence, in the next place, I must take care, lest
perchance I inconsiderately substitute some other object in room
of what is properly myself, and thus wander from truth, even in that
knowledge (cognition) which I hold to be of all others the most certain
and evident. For this reason, I will now consider anew what I formerly
believed myself to be, before I entered on the present train of thought;
and of my previous opinion I will retrench all that can in the least
be invalidated by the grounds of doubt I have adduced, in order that
there may at length remain nothing but what is certain and indubitable.

05 —

What then did I formerly think I was? Undoubtedly I judged that
I was a man. But what is a man? Shall I say a rational animal? Assuredly
not; for it would be necessary forthwith to inquire into what is meant
by animal, and what by rational, and thus, from a single question,
I should insensibly glide into others, and these more difficult than the
first; nor do I now possess enough of leisure to warrant me in wasting
my time amid subtleties of this sort. I prefer here to attend to the
thoughts that sprung up of themselves in my mind, and were inspired
by my own nature alone, when I applied myself to the consideration of
what I was. In the first place, then, I thought that I possessed a coun-
tenance, hands, arms, and all the fabric of members that appears in a

— **04**

Holy shit, okay. That's great, because it gives me *something.* But I guess even though I know I exist, I don't know much else about myself, but still. I mean, my body could still be an illusion, and maybe I'm a brain in a vat somewhere or a mind outside of space or I'm in the middle of pledge week and things are getting *seriously* out of hand. My senses and my memories still aren't reliable. Wouldn't it be nice to live in a world where everything is normal and I'm just a dude on Spring Break who fucked up once? But no, proving I exist is just like finding someone's online dating profile. It proves that there's *someone* out there, but it also suggests a bunch of shit that's maybe too good to be true. I *could* just trust my senses and my memories, but I've been burned that way before, and it would be stupid to trust that shit a second time. To make sure I don't make that rookie mistake, I'm going to go back over everything I think about myself and see if I can really be sure about any of it.

— **05**

So what do I think of myself? I mean, obviously, first thing that comes to mind, I'm a bro. Okay, what the fuck is a bro? What does it *mean,* deep down, to be a bro? A smart, handsome dude who likes to *party?* But what the fuck is a party? It requires this whole clusterfuck of beliefs about other people and music and when it's okay to cry and which mixers go with what liquors, and I can't be sure about *any* of that shit. And being *handsome* requires that I have a body, and who the fuck knows whether those even exist? And *smart?* What makes me *smart?* That I always cheat off the right kid, even though that kid might not even exist? Any definition of myself that I come up with is going to raise a bunch more questions than it answers, so a top-down approach won't work.

corpse, and which I called by the name of body. It further occurred to me that I was nourished, that I walked, perceived, and thought, and all those actions I referred to the soul; but what the soul itself was I either did not stay to consider, or, if I did, I imagined that it was something extremely rare and subtile, like wind, or flame, or ether, spread through my grosser parts. As regarded the body, I did not even doubt of its nature, but thought I distinctly knew it, and if I had wished to describe it according to the notions I then entertained, I should have explained myself in this manner: By body I understand all that can be terminated by a certain figure; that can be comprised in a certain place, and so fill a certain space as therefrom to exclude every other body; that can be perceived either by touch, sight, hearing, taste, or smell; that can be moved in different ways, not indeed of itself, but by something foreign to it by which it is touched [and from which it receives the impression]; for the power of self-motion, as likewise that of perceiving and thinking, I held as by no means pertaining to the nature of body; on the contrary, I was somewhat astonished to find such faculties existing in some bodies.

06 —

But [as to myself, what can I now say that I am], since I suppose there exists an extremely powerful, and, if I may so speak, malignant being, whose whole endeavors are directed toward deceiving me? Can I affirm that I possess any one of all those attributes of which I have lately spoken as belonging to the nature of body? After attentively considering them in my own mind, I find none of them that can properly be said to belong to myself. To recount them were idle and tedious. Let us pass, then, to the attributes of the soul. The first mentioned were the powers of nutrition and walking; but, if it be true that I have no body, it is true likewise that I am capable neither of walking nor of being nourished. Perception is another attribute of the soul; but perception too is impossible without the body; besides, I have frequent-

So rather than starting with definitions of my identity, I'll just go with whatever pops into my head when I think of "myself." What's the *first thing* I think about when I consider me?... "Holy shit what a fucking incredible body." Boom. There it is. I mean, this body is fucking chiseled. You can tell exactly where my body starts and ends, and it really fills the space. It's the kind of body that says "HEY I'M STANDING HERE" and I fucking know you can see it, you can't just walk through it goddammit, you have to acknowledge it and say something and you can try to push it out of the way but it's not going anywhere on its own, so deal with it. I'm not just a big-dicked hunk of meat, okay? My body doesn't move on its own. I'm in here! A soul lives in this body and moves it, a soul that sees shit and decides how to react and that is perfectly capable of making this body move in all kinds of ways and make all kinds of catches lots of fathers would be very proud of. What do I think of when I think of my identity? I think of myself as a mind with needs and feelings and opinions and thoughts, things that a hunk of meat could never have on its own, OKAY DAD? That's what the fuck I think of when I think about my identity.

— **06**

Shit. Anyway, that's what I used to think of myself, but it turns out almost none of that shit is important. There's this whole possible evil demon situation from yesterday going on, and maybe my body doesn't even exist, but even if my body is just an illusion, I know *I* still exist. So that means, as far as I know, none of that shit about my strong, handsome body is part of *the real me.* What about all those cool sweet powers that my soul has? A lot of them depended on having a body, like my ability to drive 320 yards off the tee. If I can't be sure I even *have* a body, obviously I can't be sure I have any powers to *move* my body. Even the ability to *perceive an outside world* depends on me *having a body to perceive it with.* So none of those mind-body powers, even the power of perceiving with my senses, are part of my true identity. *Nothing* that requires a body is part of my

ly, during sleep, believed that I perceived objects which I afterward observed I did not in reality perceive. Thinking is another attribute of the soul; and here I discover what properly belongs to myself. This alone is inseparable from me. I am—I exist: this is certain; but how often? As often as I think; for perhaps it would even happen, if I should wholly cease to think, that I should at the same time altogether cease to be. I now admit nothing that is not necessarily true. I am therefore, precisely speaking, only a thinking thing, that is, a mind (*mens sive animus*), understanding, or reason, terms whose signification was before unknown to me. I am, however, a real thing, and really existent; but what thing? The answer was, a thinking thing.

07 —

The question now arises, am I aught besides? I will stimulate my imagination with a view to discover whether I am not still something more than a thinking being. Now it is plain I am not the assemblage of members called the human body; I am not a thin and penetrating air diffused through all these members, or wind, or flame, or vapor, or breath, or any of all the things I can imagine; for I supposed that all these were not, and, without changing the supposition, I find that I still feel assured of my existence. But it is true, perhaps, that those very things which I suppose to be non-existent, because they are un-known to me, are not in truth different from myself whom I know. This is a point I cannot determine, and do not now enter into any dis-pute regarding it. I can only judge of things that are known to me: I am conscious that I exist, and I who know that I exist inquire into what I am. It is, however, perfectly certain that the knowledge of my exis-tence, thus precisely taken, is not dependent on things, the existence of which is as yet unknown to me: and consequently it is not depen-dent on any of the things I can feign in imagination. Moreover, the phrase itself, I frame an image (*effingo*), reminds me of my error; for I should in truth frame one if I were to imagine myself to be anything,

identity. The only thing that's left is: I think. I have thoughts and desires and resentments, and there's no way to doubt those, even if can doubt the things I think *about* or have resentments *toward*. So that's what I know about what I *really am*: I'm a thinking thing. That's part of the real me.

WHAT MAKES OUR HERO SO SURE THAT ALL THAT STUFF IN 06 IS NOT PART OF HIS IDENTITY?

— **07**

I'm trying to imagine what else there could be that is part of my true self, but I'm not coming up with anything. Anything I can picture existing, I can also picture not existing, and either way I know that I still exist. So none of the bodies I can imagine have to exist for *me* to exist. That's all imagination is: picturing shit, more vividly than just *thinking* of it. But I can only picture *bodies*; it doesn't make sense to try to *picture* my mind. I just end up picturing like a weird ghost or something? So *maybe* I need a body in order to exist, but how the fuck would I even figure that out? Whatever, it's not super important: right now all I care about is figuring shit out for certain, and I *can* be certain I exist, even if literally not one single thing I *imagine*, like a body, exists anywhere at all. Picturing *additional shit* after I figure that out is like saying, "Hey I'm pretty sure I got it, but lemme drop acid real quick, just to be safe. Acid always clears shit up for me." Acid trips are fun, but that's just not what I fucking need right now. What I need is to knock it off with these "imagination" shenanigans and get back to being more careful.

since to imagine is nothing more than to contemplate the figure or image of a corporeal thing; but I already know that I exist, and that it is possible at the same time that all those images, and in general all that relates to the nature of body, are merely dreams [or chimeras]. From this I discover that it is not more reasonable to say, I will excite my imagination that I may know more distinctly what I am, than to express myself as follows: I am now awake, and perceive something real; but because my perception is not sufficiently clear, I will of express purpose go to sleep that my dreams may represent to me the object of my perception with more truth and clearness. And, therefore, I know that nothing of all that I can embrace in imagination belongs to the knowledge which I have of myself, and that there is need to recall with the utmost care the mind from this mode of thinking, that it may be able to know its own nature with perfect distinctness.

08 —

But what, then, am I? A thinking thing, it has been said. But what is a thinking thing? It is a thing that doubts, understands, [conceives], affirms, denies, wills, refuses; that imagines also, and perceives.

09 —

Assuredly it is not little, if all these properties belong to my nature. But why should they not belong to it? Am I not that very being who now doubts of almost everything; who, for all that, understands and conceives certain things; who affirms one alone as true, and denies the others; who desires to know more of them, and does not wish to be deceived; who imagines many things, sometimes even despite his will; and is likewise percipient of many, as if through the medium of the senses. Is there nothing of all this as true as that I am, even although I should be always dreaming, and although he who gave me being employed all his ingenuity to deceive me? Is there also any one of

WHY DOES OUR HERO CONCLUDE THAT HIS IMAGINATION HAS NOTHING
TO OFFER HIM RIGHT NOW?

_____

_____

_____

_____

_____

_____

_____

_____

_____

_____

_____

_____

_____

— **08**

So, alright. Where does that put me? I know that I exist and that I am a
thinking thing. I *know for sure* that my essential nature includes thinking
and all the shit that comes with it: doubting, understanding, conceiving,
having great fuckin' ideas all the time, all that shit. You know, thinking?

— **09**

Okay, this is cool. I started out today knowing fucking *nothing*, and then
I got my own existence. Now I might know not only my own existence,
but also what kind of thing I am. That's *two* things I know, and honestly, I
don't see how I could be wrong here. Which is good, because that's the
entire point—to only believe shit that absolutely can't be wrong. Here I
am, right now, at this very moment, thinking and imagining and perceiving and doubting. I can imagine whatever I want, and it doesn't matter
whether a butt with three cheeks *actually exists* or not; what matters is
that I exist to imagine it. And sure, this beach and this cooler and my bros
could all be an illusion, but it doesn't matter whether the perceptions I

these attributes that can be properly distinguished from my thought, or that can be said to be separate from myself? For it is of itself so evident that it is I who doubt, I who understand, and I who desire, that it is here unnecessary to add anything by way of rendering it more clear. And I am as certainly the same being who imagines; for although it may be (as I before supposed) that nothing I imagine is true, still the power of imagination does not cease really to exist in me and to form part of my thought. In fine, I am the same being who perceives, that is, who apprehends certain objects as by the organs of sense, since, in truth, I see light, hear a noise, and feel heat. But it will be said that these presentations are false, and that I am dreaming. Let it be so. At all events it is certain that I seem to see light, hear a noise, and feel heat; this cannot be false, and this is what in me is properly called perceiving (*sentire*), which is nothing else than thinking.

10 —

From this I begin to know what I am with somewhat greater clearness and distinctness than heretofore. But, nevertheless, it still seems to me, and I cannot help believing, that corporeal things, whose images are formed by thought [which fall under the senses], and are examined by the same, are known with much greater distinctness than that I know not what part of myself which is not imaginable; although, in truth, it may seem strange to say that I know and comprehend with greater distinctness things whose existence appears to me doubtful, that are unknown, and do not belong to me, than others of whose reality I am persuaded, that are known to me, and appertain to my proper nature; in a word, than myself. But I see clearly what is the state of the case. My mind is apt to wander, and will not yet submit to be restrained within the limits of truth. Let us therefore leave the mind to itself once more, and, according to it every kind of liberty [permit it to consider the objects that appear to it from without], in order that, having afterward withdrawn it from these gently and opportunely [and

have are *true* or not; what's important is that I am in fact having these perceptions. It's like, "Is this movie based on a true story?" Bro who the fuck cares, either way I know I'm the kind of thing that can watch a movie.

WHY IS IT IMPORTANT THAT OUR HERO HAS THOUGHTS, EVEN IF THOSE THOUGHTS ARE FALSE?

———————————————————————————

———————————————————————————

———————————————————————————

———————————————————————————

———————————————————————————

———————————————————————————

———————————————————————————

———————————————————————————

— **10**

The best part of all this is that not only do I know these two things, but that I know them about my favorite thing: me. Obviously that's the best place to start—how can I know shit about the world outside me before I know anything about myself? How could any of that external world bullshit be clearer than the thoughts in my mind? My mind is literally my very identity. I mean, yes, it's hard work to stay focused internally; part of me wants to be like, "What the fuck are you talking about, evil demons and undoubtable ideas and maybe the beach isn't real? The beach is right the fuck there. How is that not way fucking clearer than, I don't know, some ghosty-self that you can't even picture?" And yeah, I mean, it does seem a little weird, doesn't it? I'm pretty convinced that knowledge starts internally and that I have to know myself before I can know anything else, but I've been focused on my own thoughts for so long that I'm going to spend some time on all this shit outside of me, just to be sure.

fixed it on the consideration of its being and the properties it finds in itself], it may then be the more easily controlled.

11 —

Let us now accordingly consider the objects that are commonly thought to be [the most easily, and likewise] the most distinctly known, viz, the bodies we touch and see; not, indeed, bodies in general, for these general notions are usually somewhat more confused, but one body in particular. Take, for example, this piece of wax; it is quite fresh, having been but recently taken from the beehive; it has not yet lost the sweetness of the honey it contained; it still retains somewhat of the odor of the flowers from which it was gathered; its color, figure, size, are apparent (to the sight); it is hard, cold, easily handled; and sounds when struck upon with the finger. In fine, all that contributes to make a body as distinctly known as possible, is found in the one before us. But, while I am speaking, let it be placed near the fire—what remained of the taste exhales, the smell evaporates, the color changes, its figure is destroyed, its size increases, it becomes liquid, it grows hot, it can hardly be handled, and, although struck upon, it emits no sound. Does the same wax still remain after this change? It must be admitted that it does remain; no one doubts it, or judges otherwise. What, then, was it I knew with so much distinctness in the piece of wax? Assuredly, it could be nothing of all that I observed by means of the senses, since all the things that fell under taste, smell, sight, touch, and hearing are changed, and yet the same wax remains.

12 —

It was perhaps what I now think, viz, that this wax was neither the sweetness of honey, the pleasant odor of flowers, the whiteness, the figure, nor the sound, but only a body that a little before appeared to me conspicuous under these forms, and which is now perceived under others. But, to speak precisely, what is it that I imagine when I think of

— **11**

So take this hunk of board wax my bro left sitting here. Nothing confusing about wax, right? It's not like a math proof or a philosophy argument or "the mind" or anything. Just wax! Simple. It shows up to all five senses—it feels pretty hard but a little squishy, it has a bluish green color, it smells like pineapple for some fucking reason, it tastes a little weird but whatever, and it makes this nice thud sound when I flick it. But what happens when I set it down and hold my lighter up to it? It gets melty, and now literally every sense detects something different. The smell and taste are gone, the color starts to go away and the wax is easier to see through, it's not hard at all, and it makes a dull squishing sound instead of a thud. Am I sure this is the same wax that got rubbed on a surfboard and left on the beach? Yeah. I'm *totally* sure. This is *obviously* the same wax, and it would be crazy to think it's not. But how the fuck do I know that it's the same wax? It can't be through the senses, since *every piece of information the senses gave me* changed in the process, but I still perceive the same piece of wax.

11–14 IS A *REALLY* IMPORTANT PART! START SUMMARIZING HERE.

_____

_____

_____

— **12**

I mean, the hunk of wax *turned into* the puddle of wax. I saw that happen. It had one shape, and then it had another, but it was the same thing the whole time. It just has different shapes and forms that it can take on. So maybe that's it? That it flowed from one state into another, without any breaks in between?

it in this way? Let it be attentively considered, and, retrenching all that does not belong to the wax, let us see what remains. There certainly remains nothing, except something extended, flexible, and movable. But what is meant by flexible and movable? Is it not that I imagine that the piece of wax, being round, is capable of becoming square, or of passing from a square into a triangular figure? Assuredly such is not the case, because I conceive that it admits of an infinity of similar changes; and I am, moreover, unable to compass this infinity by imagination, and consequently this conception which I have of the wax is not the product of the faculty of imagination. But what now is this extension? Is it not also unknown? for it becomes greater when the wax is melted, greater when it is boiled, and greater still when the heat increases; and I should not conceive [clearly and] according to truth, the wax as it is, if I did not suppose that the piece we are considering admitted even of a wider variety of extension than I ever imagined, I must, therefore, admit that I cannot even comprehend by imagination what the piece of wax is, and that it is the mind alone (*mens, Lat., entendement, F.*) which perceives it. I speak of one piece in particular; for as to wax in general, this is still more evident. But what is the piece of wax that can be perceived only by the [understanding or] mind? It is certainly the same which I see, touch, imagine; and, in fine, it is the same which, from the beginning, I believed it to be. But (and this it is of moment to observe) the perception of it is neither an act of sight, of touch, nor of imagination, and never was either of these, though it might formerly seem so, but is simply an intuition (*inspectio*) of the mind, which may be imperfect and confused, as it formerly was, or very clear and distinct, as it is at present, according as the attention is more or less directed to the elements which it contains, and of which it is composed.

If that's the explanation, then the only constant is *some body* that is flexible and movable and extended in space. How do I know this "continuous body" that can mysteriously shapeshift is still the same thing? How the fuck does my mind *hold on* to this thing if all the sensory shit keeps changing? Maybe I'm using my imagination to keep up with it?

That can't be it. It can't just be the imagination, because I understand some shit about this wax that the imagination doesn't explain. I know this ball of wax can have like a million different shapes, but I'm sure as shit not *imagining all one million shapes*. I also know it can have a bunch of different sizes, especially when I heat it up or cool it down, and I'm not, like, *picturing a bunch of different sizes*. The imagination doesn't cover nearly enough territory to explain how I know anything about this ball of wax. And that's just for this one fucking piece of wax! So the imagination isn't even *close* to explaining how the fuck I have this idea of *wax in general*, like just the abstract concept of "wax." No, I understand the idea of wax just by applying my mind to it. Even *perceiving the external world* is a totally mental process that happens with pure reason, my intellect, instead of the senses or the imagination.

So it's not that the wax *doesn't exist* or that *it isn't what I thought it was, after all*. It's definitely wax, just as I suspected the whole time. But I didn't use my senses or my imagination to "hold on" to, or perceive, the idea of the wax; it was a totally mental process. My intellect is what held on to the idea of the wax. Sometimes my grip isn't very strong, and I get this confused idea of wax that's only sort of clear; other times I can really grab on and develop a clear and distinct idea. Either way, my mind is doing all the work; my senses aren't contributing shit.

13 —

But, meanwhile, I feel greatly astonished when I observe [the weakness of my mind, and] its proneness to error. For although, without at all giving expression to what I think, I consider all this in my own mind, words yet occasionally impede my progress, and I am almost led into error by the terms of ordinary language. We say, for example, that we see the same wax when it is before us, and not that we judge it to be the same from its retaining the same color and figure: whence I should forthwith be disposed to conclude that the wax is known by the act of sight, and not by the intuition of the mind alone, were it not for the analogous instance of human beings passing on in the street below, as observed from a window. In this case I do not fail to say that I see the men themselves, just as I say that I see the wax; and yet what do I see from the window beyond hats and cloaks that might cover artificial machines, whose motions might be determined by springs? But I judge that there are human beings from these appearances, and thus I comprehend, by the faculty of judgment alone which is in the mind, what I believed I saw with my eyes.

14 —

The man who makes it his aim to rise to knowledge superior to the common, ought to be ashamed to seek occasions of doubting from the vulgar forms of speech: instead, therefore, of doing this, I shall proceed with the matter in hand, and inquire whether I had a clearer and more perfect perception of the piece of wax when I first saw it, and when I thought I knew it by means of the external sense itself, or, at all events, by the common sense (*sensus communis*), as it is called, that is, by the imaginative faculty; or whether I rather apprehend it more clearly at present, after having examined with greater care, both what

— **13**

How did I fuck that up for so long? Maybe the problem is with language. I'm over here working my ass off to discover the true nature of reality and I keep running into these really complicated ideas like "perceiving wax," which is this complex process of seeing a piece of wax and then taking what my senses pass me and assessing the shape and color of what I see and *then*, based on those factors, making the judgment that it is probably the *same* wax as the wax I saw before, but no one ever talks about that whole process. Language takes this crazy story with a lot of different steps and important details and compresses it down into "Oh, sure, I see that this is the same piece of wax as before." After a lifetime of using such simple language, I forget that we're describing a bunch of complicated shit with it, and I'm just like "If I remember correctly, perceiving is pretty simple, right?" And then I remember that oh, shit, there are lots of cases where what I perceive is *not* the same thing as what I see! Like right now, I perceive some kids walking along the beach with towels over their heads, even though my senses are like "Well, there go some towels with shitty little legs sticking out!" Even though my senses are giving me a pretty limited picture, I can tell those are kids and not demon towel robots or whatever. So perception has to be something beyond the senses, something the mind handles on its own.

— **14**

Maybe packing complicated processes into simple language works for everyday bullshitting, but everyday bullshitting is *exactly* what I'm trying to get past here. Did I have a clearer idea of the wax back when I just watched my bro wax up his board and then didn't bother to think any further? Or is it clearer now that I've thought carefully about the wax and about what it even means to *know* something? Obviously I understand it better now that I've gotten beyond just the way the wax looks. OBVIOUSLY. Who the fuck could say otherwise? I mean, seriously, what the fuck did my senses tell me, really? Literally nothing an idiot dog couldn't

it is, and in what way it can be known. It would certainly be ridiculous to entertain any doubt on this point. For what, in that first perception, was there distinct? What did I perceive which any animal might not have perceived? But when I distinguish the wax from its exterior forms, and when, as if I had stripped it of its vestments, I consider it quite naked, it is certain, although some error may still be found in my judgment, that I cannot, nevertheless, thus apprehend it without possessing a human mind.

But finally, what shall I say of the mind itself, that is, of myself? For as yet I do not admit that I am anything but mind. What, then! I who seem to possess so distinct an apprehension of the piece of wax, do I not know myself, both with greater truth and certitude, and also much more distinctly and clearly? For if I judge that the wax exists because I see it, it assuredly follows, much more evidently, that I myself am or exist, for the same reason: for it is possible that what I see may not in truth be wax, and that I do not even possess eyes with which to see anything; but it cannot be that when I see, or, which comes to the same thing, when I think I see, I myself who think am nothing. So likewise, if I judge that the wax exists because I touch it, it will still also follow that I am; and if I determine that my imagination, or any other cause, whatever it be, persuades me of the existence of the wax, I will still draw the same conclusion. And what is here remarked of the piece of wax, is applicable to all the other things that are external to me. And further, if the [notion or] perception of wax appeared to me more precise and distinct, after that not only sight and touch, but many other causes besides, rendered it manifest to my apprehension, with how much greater distinctness must I now know myself, since all the reasons that contribute to the knowledge of the nature of wax, or of any body whatever, manifest still better the nature of my mind? And there are besides so many other things in the mind itself that contribute

have *also* known about the wax. Do I know more about the wax than a dog right now? Yeah. Yeah I do. Do I know the wax perfectly? No, and maybe I'm still making *some* mistake, but the only way I could even come this far, or hope to go any further, is by having and using my human mind.

FINISH SUMMARIZING 11–14.

— **15**

So now we've come full circle—we're right back to "I could totally be fucking all this shit up, but no matter what I have a mind." I was really worried about how obvious the external world seems! I guess I thought maybe if my body was sweet enough, my *true self* would be a body, rather than what I ended up being, which is a mind. But at this point even the external world makes me think that my mind is my true self. Either I'm seeing this wax and understanding it with my mind (and so I exist and I'm a mind), or I'm being deceived and there is no wax (and so I exist and I'm a mind that's being deceived). Wax, beach, solo cup, whatever: if I'm seeing it, one way or another it proves my own existence.

In fact, pretty much no matter how I approach the wax, I'll learn more about myself than about the wax. Every single reason I have to believe the wax exists—I see it, I can imagine rubbing it all over a butt, I can think about it in my secret times—all of those reasons are even *stronger* reasons to think that *I* exist. Which, I mean, holy shit, right? How many fucking ways do I even need to know that I exist and I'm a mind?

WHY WAS 11–14 IMPORTANT? HOW DO THEY FIT IN CONTEXT?

to the illustration of its nature, that those dependent on the body, to which I have here referred, scarcely merit to be taken into account.

16   —

But, in conclusion, I find I have insensibly reverted to the point I desired; for, since it is now manifest to me that bodies themselves are not properly perceived by the senses nor by the faculty of imagination, but by the intellect alone; and since they are not perceived because they are seen and touched, but only because they are understood [or rightly comprehended by thought], I readily discover that there is nothing more easily or clearly apprehended than my own mind. But because it is difficult to rid one's self so promptly of an opinion to which one has been long accustomed, it will be desirable to tarry for some time at this stage, that, by long continued meditation, I may more deeply impress upon my memory this new knowledge.

— **16**

Oh! This also takes care of that thing I was worried about earlier, where I thought maybe my senses were more reliable than my intellect because of all this shit right in front of me that I perceive. But now I know that my senses aren't involved at all with proper perception, and neither is the imagination: the intellect handles proper perception, too. And since the intellect is how I know about *everything*, there's nothing I can be more sure of than that I exist and that my true self is a mind.

This is cool—it's very "mind over matter," and I really need to make sure it sticks.

So here's the plan: I'mma get real fucked up so that I don't worry about *anything* else and I can just totally focus on *me*. I'm really going to chisel my own existence into my mind tonight. It's gonna be great.

MEDITATION III

. . .

Of God: That He Exists.

I will now close my eyes, I will stop my ears, I will turn away my sens- es from their objects, I will even efface from my consciousness all the images of corporeal things; or at least, because this can hardly be accomplished, I will consider them as empty and false; and thus, holding converse only with myself, and closely examining my nature, I will endeavor to obtain by degrees a more intimate and familiar knowledge of myself. I am a thinking (conscious) thing, that is, a be- ing who doubts, affirms, denies, knows a few objects, and is ignorant of many,—[who loves, hates], wills, refuses, who imagines likewise, and perceives; for, as I before remarked, although the things which I perceive or imagine are perhaps nothing at all apart from me [and in themselves], I am nevertheless assured that those modes of con- sciousness which I call perceptions and imaginations, in as far only as they are modes of consciousness, exist in me.

And in the little I have said I think I have summed up all that I really know, or at least all that up to this time I was aware I knew. Now, as I am endeavoring to extend my knowledge more widely, I will use circumspection, and consider with care whether I can still discov-

MEDITATION III

. . .

Of God: That He Exists.

— 01

Yesterday I at least managed to prove my own existence to myself, and I thought maybe between that and a night of going real hard I could shake it off, but there's just so much shit I don't know about yet, and the harder I raged the more I wondered if any of it was real. So I'm going to really block out the external world, toss on these shades and put in my headphones and assume that all my thoughts about the external world are false. At least I know that I exist, and if I had to pick one thing to be real, I guess I would have picked me, so that's nice. Actually, I guess I know even a little bit more than that: I know I exist, but I also know that I *think* and *perceive* and *imagine*; you wouldn't guess it from all those hours I spent in the gym, but it turns out the core of my identity is *thinking*.

— 02

It would be great to know more stuff than just my own existence and thoughts, which is all stuff that exists *within me*. Even my own existence, I only know because... well, after thinking about it real hard, it's clear that I exist—it's not conceptually fuzzy at all. I know what it means to say that

er in myself anything further which I have not yet hitherto observed. I am certain that I am a thinking thing; but do I not therefore likewise know what is required to render me certain of a truth? In this first knowledge, doubtless, there is nothing that gives me assurance of its truth except the clear and distinct perception of what I affirm, which would not indeed be sufficient to give me the assurance that what I say is true, if it could ever happen that anything I thus clearly and distinctly perceived should prove false; and accordingly it seems to me that I may now take as a general rule, that all that is very clearly and distinctly apprehended (conceived) is true.

03 —

Nevertheless I before received and admitted many things as wholly certain and manifest, which yet I afterward found to be doubtful. What, then, were those? They were the earth, the sky, the stars, and all the other objects which I was in the habit of perceiving by the senses. But what was it that I clearly [and distinctly] perceived in them? Nothing more than that the ideas and the thoughts of those objects were presented to my mind. And even now I do not deny that these ideas are found in my mind. But there was yet another thing which I affirmed, and which, from having been accustomed to believe it, I thought I clearly perceived, although, in truth, I did not perceive it at all; I mean the existence of objects external to me, from which those ideas proceeded, and to which they had a perfect resemblance; and it was here I was mistaken, or if I judged correctly, this assuredly was not to be traced to any knowledge I possessed (the force of my perception, Lat.).

04 —

But when I considered any matter in arithmetic and geometry, that was very simple and easy, as, for example, that two and three added

I exist, and I can see how my own existence is definitely, absolutely true. It's also really distinct to me, like there's no alternative that I could be getting it mixed up with and no leftover questions where I'm like, "Well I exist as long as I *also* have a body, and I *probably* have a body, right?" Instead, it stands completely on its own. It's this clear, distinct perception that I can't get away from once I have it. I don't even fucking know where I'd start doubting it.

Since having this clear, distinct perception is enough to prove to myself that I exist, it also tells me how to go about discovering more shit: only trust clear, distinct perceptions, because I can trust those even if I can't trust anything else.

— **03**

Wait, but isn't this beach and all this other shit pretty clear and distinct? No, what's clear and distinct is that I *think* I see a beach, but that's not a huge deal. Obviously it feels like I'm looking at a beach, but I don't know if that means there actually *is* a beach out there, or even if "out there" exists at all. I *do* know that the thoughts I'm having are in me, but I can't just rush back to trusting that they correspond to the external world at all.

WHAT IS THE GOAL OF THIS MEDITATION? HOW DOES IT FIT IN CONTEXT?

—————————————————————————

—————————————————————————

—————————————————————————

—————————————————————————

—————————————————————————

— **04**

What about math? 2+3=5. If 2+3≠5, I should be able to figure that out when I really think about it. Like, "Sure maybe it looks like 5 when you're

together make five, and things of this sort, did I not view them with
at least sufficient clearness to warrant me in affirming their truth?
Indeed, if I afterward judged that we ought to doubt of these things,
it was for no other reason than because it occurred to me that a
God might perhaps have given me such a nature as that I should be
deceived, even respecting the matters that appeared to me the most
evidently true. But as often as this preconceived opinion of the sovereign power of a God presents itself to my mind, I am constrained to
admit that it is easy for him, if he wishes it, to cause me to err, even in
matters where I think I possess the highest evidence; and, on the other hand, as often as I direct my attention to things which I think I apprehend with great clearness, I am so persuaded of their truth that
I naturally break out into expressions such as these: Deceive me who
may, no one will yet ever be able to bring it about that I am not, so
long as I shall be conscious that I am, or at any future time cause it to
be true that I have never been, it being now true that I am, or make
two and three more or less than five, in supposing which, and other
like absurdities, I discover a manifest contradiction. And in truth, as
I have no ground for believing that Deity is deceitful, and as, indeed, I
have not even considered the reasons by which the existence of a Deity of any kind is established, the ground of doubt that rests only on
this supposition is very slight, and, so to speak, metaphysical. But, that
I may be able wholly to remove it, I must inquire whether there is a God,
as soon as an opportunity of doing so shall present itself; and if I find
that there is a God, I must examine likewise whether he can be a deceiver; for, without the knowledge of these two truths, I do not see that I can
ever be certain of anything. And that I may be enabled to examine this
without interrupting the order of meditation I have proposed to myself
[which is, to pass by degrees from the notions that I shall find first in
my mind to those I shall afterward discover in it], it is necessary at this
stage to divide all my thoughts into certain classes, and to consider in
which of these classes truth and error are, strictly speaking, to be found.

not paying attention, but look again, fuckjaw. Do the math out all the way. It's 8." But no, the more I think about it, the more I want to shout from the rooftops, "HEY EVERYBODY, **2+3=5** AND I DON'T CARE WHO KNOWS IT." Just like I'm not sure where to start doubting "I exist," I don't know where to start doubting "2+3=5."

The only difference... oh. Alright. Okay. The difference between "I exist" and "2+3=5" is that not even an all-powerful God could make me wrong about my own existence, because I have to exist to be fooled. But I guess a God like that *could* fuck with me every time I try to do math, like He's just *hiding* an extra number or something. Why would He do that? I don't fucking know, but He *could* do it, and that's all I need. So I know that really, truly, 2+3=5, or there's some incredibly powerful Being lying to me for some idiot reason, *or* it could be that I'm just fucking stupid. Great. Fuck. So now I have to figure out if God is real *and* whether He's fucking with me? How do I go about *proving the existence and honesty of God?* Fuck. I am so far down this fucking rabbit hole. Since all I know about is these thoughts in my head, I guess the best place I should figure out what *kinds* of thoughts I have, so I can decide what it even *means* for a thought to be *true or false.*

WHY IS THE DIFFERENCE BETWEEN OUR HERO'S PERCEPTION OF THE BEACH AND THE BEACH ITSELF IMPORTANT?

05 —

Of my thoughts some are, as it were, images of things, and to these alone properly belongs the name IDEA; as when I think [represent to my mind] a man, a chimera, the sky, an angel or God. Others, again, have certain other forms; as when I will, fear, affirm, or deny, I always, indeed, apprehend something as the object of my thought, but I also embrace in thought something more than the representation of the object; and of this class of thoughts some are called volitions or affections, and others judgments.

06 —

Now, with respect to ideas, if these are considered only in themselves, and are not referred to any object beyond them, they cannot, properly speaking, be false; for, whether I imagine a goat or chimera, it is not less true that I imagine the one than the other. Nor need we fear that falsity may exist in the will or affections; for, although I may desire objects that are wrong, and even that never existed, it is still true that I desire them. There thus only remain our judgments, in which we must take diligent heed that we be not deceived. But the chief and most ordinary error that arises in them consists in judging that the ideas which are in us are like or conformed to the things that are external to us; for assuredly, if we but considered the ideas themselves as certain modes of our thought (consciousness), without referring them to anything beyond, they would hardly afford any occasion of error.

OUTLINE THE THREE KINDS OF THOUGHT FROM 05 HERE.

— **05**

Here's one kind of thought that I have: I've got these *ideas* like "myself" and "hangover" and "entire body" and "tremendous pain," and these ideas are sort of like *images* or mental representations of things.

But I also have thoughts that aren't images *of* things, but are judgements *about* things, like "Here's something that's true about me: I have a hangover, and my entire body hurts." Or "If I smell tequila, I will certainly vomit." Other times, instead of making judgements, I'm *feeling a way* about a thing, like "I hope I die soon so this hangover goes away," or "Ugh, ew, tequila, fuck me, get away, fucking tequila, *hurp.*"

— **06**

Ideas themselves can't be *true or false*; like, even if I have an idea of some weird shit like *Front Butt, The Butt That Goes In Front,* the idea itself isn't *false.* It's just this weird funny idea.

Emotions can't be true or false, either, even though they're *about* things. If I'm like, "Actually I want to touch a *Front Butt,*" my bro might be like, "What? Bro that's fucked up." And it's like, I know that, you think I don't know that? But it doesn't mean my desire is *literally false.* It just means I'm into some weird shit, maybe. Or even if I'm wrong about tequila making me vomit, the thought "Aaaaaahhhh oh no tequila" isn't *false.*

But I *can* be wrong about whether the smell of tequila will make me vomit, because when I make *judgments* about things, those *can* be true or false. Likewise, when I think "*Front Butts* exist out there in the world," that really *is* literally false. In fact, I make judgments like "these ideas I have are pictures of things that exist outside of me" *all the time,* even though it turns out I *totally* can't be sure about that at all. Of course, if I just make judgments about ideas formally, as *just ideas,* without worrying about what they're supposed to be images *of,* that's way harder to fuck up. So I guess I'll start there.

07 —

But among these ideas, some appear to me to be innate, others adventitious, and others to be made by myself (factitious); for, as I have the power of conceiving what is called a thing, or a truth, or a thought, it seems to me that I hold this power from no other source than my own nature; but if I now hear a noise, if I see the sun, or if I feel heat, I have all along judged that these sensations proceeded from certain objects existing out of myself; and, in fine, it appears to me that sirens, hippogryphs, and the like, are inventions of my own mind. But I may even perhaps come to be of opinion that all my ideas are of the class which I call adventitious, or that they are all innate, or that they are all factitious; for I have not yet clearly discovered their true origin.

08 —

What I have here principally to do is to consider, with reference to those that appear to come from certain objects without me, what grounds there are for thinking them like these objects. The first of these grounds is that it seems to me I am so taught by nature; and the second that I am conscious that those ideas are not dependent on my will, and therefore not on myself, for they are frequently presented to me against my will, as at present, whether I will or not, I feel heat; and I am thus persuaded that this sensation or idea (*sensum vel ideam*) of heat is produced in me by something different from myself, *viz.*, by the heat of the fire by which I sit. And it is very reasonable to suppose that this object impresses me with its own likeness rather than any other thing.

WHAT KIND OF IDEA IS OUR HERO GOING TO HUNT FOR?

— **07**

Where did all these ideas inside of me come from? I think there are only like three options: they came from someone or something outside of me, I made them up myself, or they've literally just always been there. I don't know if I got any idea from outside, but *maybe* the idea of a beach came from some beach that's really out there. On the other hand, I know I invented at least *some* ideas myself, like "keg-dragoning" and "beach ball beer pong." But then I have this idea of "thoughts," which I don't think I *invented*; the idea of a thought probably just came directly from my nature as a thinking thing; it was always there.

Right? I think that covers everything, but maybe *all* my ideas came from the outside or maybe I invented *all* of them or maybe I've always had *all* these ideas. I don't know.

— **08**

But *if* the idea of a beach—or any of my ideas, really—corresponds to something real that exists outside of me, that would mean there really *is* something else out there besides just me and my thoughts. So ideas are like pictures, but do they *resemble* the things they come from?

When I'm composing a dick pic, I'm always like, "Hmmm, what's the best angle here? How can I get the most out of the lighting?" There's no guarantee my picture will be an *accurate* representation; why should ideas be any different? How can I be sure my idea of the beach comes from a thing that *actually looks like my idea of a beach?* On one hand, that's *really* hard to doubt. It seems obvious that, like, "no shit, the idea of a beach is just a picture of the beach. What else could it be a picture of?"

Also, it's not like I'm making these ideas up *wishfully.* I mean sure, sometimes maybe I want an ice cold beer so bad that I'm *willing the idea to appear.* Fine. But what about this, fuck, what about this sunburn I'm developing? *That's* not any idea I *want* to be having, and yet here we are. If there isn't any actual sunburn like this out there in the world, and I'm

09 —

But I must consider whether these reasons are sufficiently strong and convincing. When I speak of being taught by nature in this matter, I understand by the word nature only a certain spontaneous impetus that impels me to believe in a resemblance between ideas and their objects, and not a natural light that affords a knowledge of its truth. But these two things are widely different; for what the natural light shows to be true can be in no degree doubtful, as, for example, that I am because I doubt, and other truths of the like kind; inasmuch as I possess no other faculty whereby to distinguish truth from error, which can teach me the falsity of what the natural light declares to be true, and which is equally trustworthy; but with respect to [seemingly] natural impulses, I have observed, when the question related to the choice of right or wrong in action, that they frequently led me to take the worse part; nor do I see that I have any better ground for following them in what relates to truth and error.

10 —

Then, with respect to the other reason, which is that because these ideas do not depend on my will, they must arise from objects existing without me, I do not find it more convincing than the former, for just as those natural impulses, of which I have lately spoken, are found in me, notwithstanding that they are not always in harmony with my will, so likewise it may be that I possess some power not sufficiently known to myself capable of producing ideas without the aid of external objects, and, indeed, it has always hitherto appeared to me that they are formed during sleep, by some power of this nature, without the aid of aught external.

not making the idea up myself, where else could that come from? A wet towel that gives the feeling of sunburn? That seems fucking stupid.

— **09**

On the other hand, maybe it's not so easy after all. It *seems* obvious that ideas resemble their source, but it also *seemed* obvious that the dude I saw at the bar was Paul Rabil, and look where *that* got me. Meanwhile, by now it *is* obvious that I exist, but that was only after a whole day thinking about that shit carefully and really understanding why that had to be true. I only got to be smug about my own existence because I straight up ran out of ways to doubt it; I thought about whether or not I exist as carefully as possible and I proved it to myself using my reason. It's not like I have an abacus or some shit in the back of my brain I can use to *double-check* it, right? Thinking carefully and paying close attention is the very best I can do. Right now though, I'm just like "well obviously, ideas resemble their source, right?" without any of that carefully thinking business. "That's super easy to believe" is a stupid reason to believe something.

— **10**

And I guess I could be making this shitty sunburn up myself, even if I don't want to. I mean, I have scary-ass dreams all the time, and it's not like I want to have *those*, but they don't come from anywhere else. I don't want to have these ideas, but that doesn't make me *certain* that I'm not making them up anyway, and *certainty* is what I need.

WHAT ASSUMPTION DOES OUR HERO REJECT IN 08–10?

11 —

And, in fine, although I should grant that they proceeded from those objects, it is not a necessary consequence that they must be like them. On the contrary, I have observed, in a number of instances, that there was a great difference between the object and its idea. Thus, for example, I find in my mind two wholly diverse ideas of the sun; the one, by which it appears to me extremely small draws its origin from the senses, and should be placed in the class of adventitious ideas; the other, by which it seems to be many times larger than the whole earth, is taken up on astronomical grounds, that is, elicited from certain notions born with me, or is framed by myself in some other manner. These two ideas cannot certainly both resemble the same sun; and reason teaches me that the one which seems to have immediately emanated from it is the most unlike.

12 —

And these things sufficiently prove that hitherto it has not been from a certain and deliberate judgment, but only from a sort of blind impulse, that I believed existence of certain things different from myself, which, by the organs of sense, or by whatever other means it might be, conveyed their ideas or images into my mind [and impressed it with their likenesses].

13 —

But there is still another way of inquiring whether, of the objects whose ideas are in my mind, there are any that exist out of me. If ideas are taken in so far only as they are certain modes of consciousness, I do not remark any difference or inequality among them, and all seem, in the same manner, to proceed from myself; but, considering them as images, of which one represents one thing and another a different, it is evident that a great diversity obtains among them. For, without doubt,

— **11**

Even if I'm not making things up, like even if these ideas *do* come from something outside of me, the ideas don't have to look exactly the same as their source. I mean, take the sun, from which all true tans and sweet bods flow; one idea I have is that the sun is this tiny little circle that moves through the sky and makes me even handsomer than usual and I can use my hand to cover it if I need to see some butts more clearly. The other idea, the one I learned in science class, is that the sun is actually a giant sphere that is literally billions of times bigger than me, and I'm actually moving around *it*. Those ideas are supposed to be about the same thing, but they're so different that only one of them can really resemble the actual sun, right? And I feel like the one that I learned in science class is the one that's the *better*, more accurate one. If the sun is out there giving me the idea of a tiny sun that moves, it shows that it's totally possible for an idea to be a bad representation of its source.

— **12**

All of this shows that I didn't have good, careful, grown-ass man reasons for believing in these external objects; I was just like "oh shit I saw some mind pictures, I'll bet that's real stuff out there."

— **13**

When I consider ideas *formally,* as all the same kind of thought, no idea has any more *reality* than any other idea. They all have the same amount of *formal reality.* But ideas are also special because they're representa-tions. Ideas represent all kinds of shit, and some things have more reality in them than other things. My bros are throwing around a football, and there's a weird egg shape to the ball. Obviously, the ball itself has more formal reality than the eggy shape has; the ball is a thing with substance,

those that represent substances are something more, and contain in themselves, so to speak, more objective reality [that is, participate by representation in higher degrees of being or perfection], than those that represent only modes or accidents; and again, the idea by which I conceive a God [sovereign], eternal, infinite, [immutable], all-knowing, all-powerful, and the creator of all things that are out of himself, this, I say, has certainly in it more objective reality than those ideas by which finite substances are represented.

14 —

Now, it is manifest by the natural light that there must at least be as much reality in the efficient and total cause as in its effect; for whence can the effect draw its reality if not from its cause? And how could the cause communicate to it this reality unless it possessed it in itself? And hence it follows, not only that what is cannot be produced by what is not, but likewise that the more perfect, in other words, that which contains in itself more reality, cannot be the effect of the less perfect; and this is not only evidently true of those effects, whose reality is actual or formal, but likewise of ideas, whose reality is only considered as objective. Thus, for example, the stone that is not yet in existence, not only cannot now commence to be, unless it be produced by that which possesses in itself, formally or eminently, all that enters into its composition, [in other words, by that which contains in itself the same properties that are in the stone, or others superior to them]; and heat can only be produced in a subject that was before devoid of it, by a cause that is of an order, [degree or kind], at least as perfect as heat; and so of the others. But further, even the idea of the heat, or of the stone, cannot exist in me unless it be put there by a cause that contains, at least, as much reality as I conceive existent in the heat or in the stone for although that cause may not transmit into my idea anything of its actual or formal reality, we ought not on this account to imagine that it is less real; but we ought to consider that, [as every

and the shape is just a fucking shape. Since the ball is realer than the eggy shape, the idea representing the ball has more *objective reality* than the idea representing the eggy shape has, because the objective reality of an idea is how much reality is in whatever the idea *represents*. Likewise, I have this idea of an infinite and all-powerful, all-good God who bestows every college football game on us year after year, and that represents something way realer than one single shitty football, so the idea of God has more objective reality than the idea of a football.

— **14**

If a thing has *an amount* of reality, obviously there has to be at least as much reality in the source of that thing, right? Like, whoever made that football better have at least as much reality as the ball itself, or else where the fuck did the ball get its reality from? It's not like *shapes* can make *things*; shapes have less formal reality than things, so things can't come from them. And maybe the idea of a football came from the football itself, or maybe it came from somewhere else. Either way, an idea has some objective reality, and the source of that idea is going to need at least as much formal reality.

It's like that bouncer Marv from the other night; he's not going to let you through unless you've got a popular friend to put you on the list. If a football tries to get into Club Existence, Marv would be like, "Cool, as long as something at least as real as you puts you on the list, you can get into the club." The football can't say, "Well I got this weird egg shape to back me up, he's got *some* formal reality, and then maybe I can just borrow the rest from Nothingness?" Marv isn't having that shit; things becoming real out of Nothing is exactly the kind of metaphysical shenanigans Marv was hired to prevent.

And before an idea can exist in my mind, someone has to cover whichever is greater: its formal reality or its objective reality. So, a clear idea of a football? If a football has more reality than an idea, then anything that creates an idea of a football needs at least as much formal reality as

idea is a work of the mind], its nature is such as of itself to demand no other formal reality than that which it borrows from our consciousness, of which it is but a mode [that is, a manner or way of thinking]. But in order that an idea may contain this objective reality rather than that, it must doubtless derive it from some cause in which is found at least as much formal reality as the idea contains of objective; for, if we suppose that there is found in an idea anything which was not in its cause, it must of course derive this from nothing. But, however imperfect may be the mode of existence by which a thing is objectively [or by representation] in the understanding by its idea, we certainly cannot, for all that, allege that this mode of existence is nothing, nor, consequently, that the idea owes its origin to nothing.

15 —

Nor must it be imagined that, since the reality which considered in these ideas is only objective, the same reality need not be formally (actually) in the causes of these ideas, but only objectively: for, just as the mode of existing objectively belongs to ideas by their peculiar nature, so likewise the mode of existing formally appertains to the causes of these ideas (at least to the first and principal), by their peculiar nature. And although an idea may give rise to another idea, this regress cannot, nevertheless, be infinite; we must in the end reach a first idea, the cause of which is, as it were, the archetype in which all the reality [or perfection] that is found objectively [or by representation] in these ideas is contained formally [and in act]. I am thus clearly taught by the natural light that ideas exist in me as pictures or images, which may, in truth, readily fall short of the perfection of the objects from which they are taken, but can never contain anything greater or more perfect.

a *football itself.* Since I've got more reality than a football, I've got more than enough to cover the idea of a football. I could be like, "It's totally cool, clear idea of a football. I got you covered. You can exist in my mind now." But what if I had an idea that clearly had way more reality than I have? It would be a Big Idea. I can't be the source of Big Ideas, since I don't have enough reality to get any Big Ideas into Club Existence, and they'd have to borrow reality from Nothingness. I can't stress this enough you guys, Marv takes that shit incredibly seriously and would absolutely not let me cover a Big Idea on my own.

— **15**

I might say to Marv, "Hey Marv, can I cover objective reality with other objective reality? Can ideas be the source of other ideas?" I think he'd be like, "Sure, that's no problem, as long as you can account for the reality in that first idea." So for example let's say angels are real and they are just a little more real than I am. That means I can't be the source for a clear idea of angels. (Maybe I'd get close, since I have *almost* as much reality as an angel, but I would have a muddied picture that only kind of represents angels rather than clearly and distinctly representing them. Like maybe if I tried to derive the idea of angels myself I'd just come up with... Idris Elba but with wings and a sword and an even better jawline? I don't fucking know.) But I could maybe say, "Hey Marv, you know me, I'm *pretty* real, but also I've got this idea of God that has like an infinite amount of objective reality. Can I use that to cover the difference?" Seems like Marv would be cool with that; the idea of God has so much reality that it could easily serve as a kind of inspiration for the idea of angels. So that would get me a clearer idea of angels, but now I have to explain how I got the idea of God. How the fuck did I get an idea *that* big? I just explained the Big Idea of angels with the even Bigger Idea of God, but that just

WHY DO IDEAS HAVE BOTH OBJECTIVE AND FORMAL REALITY?
WHAT'S THE DIFFERENCE?

16 —

And in proportion to the time and care with which I examine all those matters, the conviction of their truth brightens and becomes distinct. But, to sum up, what conclusion shall I draw from it all? It is this: if the objective reality [or perfection] of any one of my ideas be such as clearly to convince me, that this same reality exists in me neither formally nor eminently, and if, as follows from this, I myself cannot be the cause of it, it is a necessary consequence that I am not alone in the world, but that there is besides myself some other being who exists as the cause of that idea; while, on the contrary, if no such idea be found in my mind, I shall have no sufficient ground of assurance of the existence of any other being besides myself, for, after a most careful search, I have, up to this moment, been unable to discover any other ground.

17 —

But, among these my ideas, besides that which represents myself, respecting which there can be here no difficulty, there is one that represents a God; others that represent corporeal and inanimate things; others angels; others animals; and, finally, there are some that represent men like myself.

moves the problem one level back. Eventually, there's going to be a Biggest Idea at the end of the chain, something too big to be explained by other ideas, and there has to be some shit with enough formal reality to cover it. Maybe ideas can have *less* reality than the thing they represent, but they sure as shit can't have *more* reality. How the fuck could the idea of something be *more* real than the thing itself? When you get to the Biggest Idea, Marv is gonna be like, "Alright, assholes, I've talked to a whole bunch of ideas tryna get into this club, but eventually something with a shitload of formal reality is going to have to speak up. What's it gonna be? You got someone famous with you or what?"

— **16**

Alright, things are starting to come together for me. So if there are any Big Ideas, they can't come from *me*, but they'd have to come from somewhere. There'd have to be something else with enough reality to cover a Big Idea. That means if I can *find* a Big Idea, I'll know there's at least *one* thing besides me, which would be great fucking news because if I *can't* find any Big Ideas, I'm stuck in this shitty position like "well, I exist, but it sure is lonely out here, just me and my ideas and Marv, who isn't real at all but is strictly an analogy."

— **17**

Here's some shit I have ideas about; maybe a Big Idea could come from one of these categories. I have an idea of God; ideas of things like bodies and footballs, angels, animals, and lastly I've got ideas of other dudes. If I can clearly and distinctly prove any of them has more objective reality than I have, it would be enough to know something exists outside of my

WHAT MAKES A BIG IDEA, AND WHY ARE THEY IMPORTANT TO OUR HERO?

....

....

....

18 —

But with respect to the ideas that represent other men, or animals, or angels, I can easily suppose that they were formed by the mingling and composition of the other ideas which I have of myself, of corporeal things, and of God, although they were, apart from myself, neither men, animals, nor angels.

WHY DON'T IDEAS THAT MIGHT HAVE MORE REALITY THAN OUR HERO QUALIFY AS BIG IDEAS?

....

....

....

19 —

And with regard to the ideas of corporeal objects, I never discovered in them anything so great or excellent which I myself did not appear capable of originating; for, by considering these ideas closely and scrutinizing them individually, in the same way that I yesterday examined the idea of wax, I find that there is but little in them that is clearly and distinctly perceived. As belonging to the class of things that are clearly apprehended, I recognize the following, viz, magnitude or extension in length, breadth, and depth; figure, which results from the termination of extension; situation, which bodies of diverse figures preserve with reference to each other; and motion or the change of situation; to which may be added substance, duration, and number. But with regard to light, colors, sounds, odors, tastes, heat, cold, and the other tactile qualities, they are thought with so much obscurity and confusion, that I cannot determine even whether they are true or

mind. If I fail with all of them, I can say goodbye to my best chance of ever knowing whether the external world exists or not, which would be shitty but I guess it would mean I could just never stop drinking because who knows if it's real enough to matter anyway?

— **18**

Pretty much right away I can tell that ideas of other people and ideas of angels won't be Big Ideas. Since I'm the realest bro, other bros aren't any realer than I am. I could totally be making up the idea of my boys Tad and Chad, Marv would be cool with that. And with angels, my idea of them isn't super clear. Like, I can't be sure I'm not just taking my idea of myself and smashing it together with like "wings and a harp and also something about God," and coming up with this muddled idea of angels that only has as much reality as I do. Or maybe my idea is clear, but I have to use the idea of God to explain it. I don't know. The point is, my ideas of angels and bros aren't good candidates for Big Ideas.

— **19**

Ideas of shit like footballs and butts, really just ideas of bodies in general, those aren't good candidates for Big Ideas either. I definitely have enough formal reality to cover all that shit. There's a huge variety of ideas that fall under the category "ideas of external bodies," but almost none of those ideas are clear and distinct. There are some things I can tell for sure about bodies, but it's only like a couple things. Take butts, for example. First, butts have size, some are bigger than others. Second, butts have shape. Third, butts are positioned relative to other bodies, so for example I'm always tryna get closer to a butt. Fourth, butts have motion, and I like the way butts move. Fifth, butts're made of stuff. Sixth, butts exist for periods of time. And finally, there are distinct quantities of butts: I can tell there are three butts over there or five butts over at so-and-so's party or such-and-such many butts in my view right now. These seven ideas are clear and distinct not just about butts, but about bodies generally.

false; in other words, whether or not the ideas I have of these qualities are in truth the ideas of real objects. For although I before remarked that it is only in judgments that formal falsity, or falsity properly so called, can be met with, there may nevertheless be found in ideas a certain material falsity, which arises when they represent what is nothing as if it were something. Thus, for example, the ideas I have of cold and heat are so far from being clear and distinct, that I am unable from them to discover whether cold is only the privation of heat, or heat the privation of cold; or whether they are or are not real qualities: and since, ideas being as it were images there can be none that does not seem to us to represent some object, the idea which represents cold as something real and positive will not improperly be called false, if it be correct to say that cold is nothing but a privation of heat; and so in other cases.

20 —

To ideas of this kind, indeed, it is not necessary that I should assign any author besides myself: for if they are false, that is, represent objects that are unreal, the natural light teaches me that they proceed from nothing; in other words, that they are in me only because something is wanting to the perfection of my nature; but if these ideas are true, yet because they exhibit to me so little reality that I cannot even distinguish the object represented from nonbeing, I do not see why I should not be the author of them.

21 —

With reference to those ideas of corporeal things that are clear and distinct, there are some which, as appears to me, might have been taken from the idea I have of myself, as those of substance, duration, number, and the like. For when I think that a stone is a substance, or a thing capable of existing of itself, and that I am likewise a substance, although I conceive that I am a thinking and non-extended thing, and

There are a lot of other ideas about bodies, though, like light, color, sound, taste, temperature, and none of that shit is clear and distinct. If the idea "bodies take up space" is like a high-res photo, the ideas of color and temperature are a blurry drunk selfie. I definitely have the ideas of heat and cold, but I can't tell which one is the absence of which. Is heat the absence of cold? Is cold the absence of heat? I don't know. Hot and cold both seem like actual things to me, but as far as I know it could just be "hot and not-hot" or "cold and not-cold."

WHAT HAPPENS IF OUR HERO CAN'T FIND A BIG IDEA?

— **20**

This shit is getting all muddled for me again, which is exactly the problem: my ideas about external bodies are pretty much just confused clusterfucks. All those ideas of external things (besides the clear and distinct seven) are too muddled, and if there's anything I've learned this week, it's that muddled ideas are my fucking specialty. If there's even the *possibility* that these ideas came from me, they're definitely not good candidates for Big Ideas.

— **21**

And I don't think those seven clear and distinct butt-facts get me anywhere, because I feel like those could all come from my idea of myself. Right? Well, I have the idea of myself being made of some sort of substance, and butts are made of a substance, too. So that fifth idea, that things are made of substances, maybe I got that from me. And since I have memories of yesterday and memories of today, maybe I can break

that the stone, on the contrary, is extended and unconscious, there being thus the greatest diversity between the two concepts, yet these two ideas seem to have this in common that they both represent substances. In the same way, when I think of myself as now existing, and recollect besides that I existed some time ago, and when I am conscious of various thoughts whose number I know, I then acquire the ideas of duration and number, which I can afterward transfer to as many objects as I please. With respect to the other qualities that go to make up the ideas of corporeal objects, viz, extension, figure, situation, and motion, it is true that they are not formally in me, since I am merely a thinking being; but because they are only certain modes of substance, and because I myself am a substance, it seems possible that they may be contained in me eminently.

WHY AREN'T THESE SEVEN IDEAS BIG IDEAS, EVEN THOUGH THEY'RE CLEAR AND DISTINCT TO OUR HERO?

---

22 —

There only remains, therefore, the idea of God, in which I must consider whether there is anything that cannot be supposed to originate with myself. By the name God, I understand a substance infinite, [eternal, immutable], independent, all-knowing, all-powerful, and by which I myself, and every other thing that exists, if any such there be, were created. But these properties are so great and excellent, that the more attentively I consider them the less I feel persuaded that the idea I have of them owes its origin to myself alone. And thus it is absolutely necessary to conclude, from all that I have before said, that God exists.

those down into "earlier" and "later" or "before" and "after." Since those memories are ideas that I could cover for, Marv would be cool with me covering the parts, too. That takes care of No. 6, the idea of butts existing in time. Since I have multiple thoughts I can count, I can really easily derive the idea of all the numbers and quantities by just counting my ideas over and over. That takes care of No. 7, quantities of butts. As for No. 1 through No. 4, those are just modes of substance, which is like "here's one way a substance can be." Substances come in a shitload of modes: sizes, shapes, places, and so on. Maybe it's enough that "modes" are substance-related things, and I am a substance. Like, "Oh, modes need substances to live in, and I'm made of a substance, so I can have ideas of modes!" Does that make sense? Maybe not, but what's important is that I can't *prove* that the idea of being egg-shaped didn't come from me, and that's what I'd need anyway. I'm trying to prove that something *else* exists, something outside my mind, and I should err on the side of assuming that ideas came from me, just to be safe. I need a real fucking good explanation as to why any idea *can't* start with me, and I don't have any explanation for why I can't just make up the idea of "being spherical" on my own without any help.

— 22

The only candidate for a Big Idea I have left is this idea of God, because fucking of *course* it would come down to this stupid God bullshit again. Great. Cool. So I have an idea of an infinite, eternal, independent, all-knowing, all-powerful Substance that created me and anything else that may or may not exist. Oh, but holy shit. Wait a second. I think ideas like "infinity" and "all-powerfulness" really are Big Ideas, ideas that couldn't have come from me. Holy fuck, if I'm right about that, it would mean God has to actually exist, since He'd be the only thing with enough formal reality to cover the objective reality contained by the *idea* of God.

23 —

For though the idea of substance be in my mind owing to this, that I myself am a substance, I should not, however, have the idea of an infinite substance, seeing I am a finite being, unless it were given me by some substance in reality infinite.

OUR HERO THINKS THE IDEA OF GOD IS A BIG IDEA, AND HE CONSIDERS AND REJECTS A BUNCH OF OBJECTIONS. LIST THEM HERE.

24 —

And I must not imagine that I do not apprehend the infinite by a true idea, but only by the negation of the finite, in the same way that I comprehend repose and darkness by the negation of motion and light: since, on the contrary, I clearly perceive that there is more reality in the infinite substance than in the finite, and therefore that in some way I possess the perception (notion) of the infinite before that of the finite, that is, the perception of God before that of myself, for how could I know that I doubt, desire, or that something is wanting to me, and that I am not wholly perfect, if I possessed no idea of a being more perfect than myself, by comparison of which I knew the deficiencies of my nature?

25 —

And it cannot be said that this idea of God is perhaps materially false, and consequently that it may have arisen from nothing [in other words, that it may exist in me from my imperfections as I before said

— **23**

Alright dude, be cool. Don't get ahead of yourself. I've already shown how I can get the ideas of "substance" and "numbers" from myself, but that doesn't apply to the idea of *infinite* substance. That's a whole different ballgame. I'm a finite being. If I tried to invent the idea of *infinite*, Marv would be like, "Oh yeah, infinite substance? What is that?" And I'd be like, "Uh... hey Marv... uh, you know, substance that's... uh... you know how I'm limited? This is like that, except the opposite." Which obviously doesn't do it for Marv. "Oh, really? Just like you, except the opposite? Alright, easy. Just tell me what it's like to be like you, except unlimited." And I'd have to say, "I... I don't know. The thing is, I'm limited. If I had enough reality to describe being unlimited, I wouldn't be limited." And Marv would say, "That's what I thought motherfucker, get to the back of the line." Marv is cruel, but he is fair.

— **24**

There are definitely *some* ideas I can get to by negating another idea, like how I understand "dark" as "not light" or "resting" as "not moving" or "fuckin' nerd" as "not a bro." But I can only do that if I'm getting to a smaller idea from a bigger one, and that's not happening here. There's more reality in infinite substance than in finite substance, so I can't get the idea of infinity from finity; I have to already have the idea of infinity somehow. I have to already have the idea of God, an infinite dude, in order to have the idea that I am a pretty-solid-but-ultimately-*finite* dude.

— **25**

Plus there's just no fucking way this idea of God is just something I made up. Maybe I made up the ideas of angels, because those ideas are some fuzzy-ass shit. But my idea of God is clear and distinct, and it clearly,

of the ideas of heat and cold, and the like: for, on the contrary, as this idea is very clear and distinct, and contains in itself more objective reality than any other, there can be no one of itself more true, or less open to the suspicion of falsity. The idea, I say, of a being supremely perfect, and infinite, is in the highest degree true; for although, perhaps, we may imagine that such a being does not exist, we cannot, nevertheless, suppose that his idea represents nothing real, as I have already said of the idea of cold. It is likewise clear and distinct in the highest degree, since whatever the mind clearly and distinctly conceives as real or true, and as implying any perfection, is contained entire in this idea. And this is true, nevertheless, although I do not comprehend the infinite, and although there may be in God an infinity of things that I cannot comprehend, nor perhaps even compass by thought in any way; for it is of the nature of the infinite that it should not be comprehended by the finite; and it is enough that I rightly understand this, and judge that all which I clearly perceive, and in which I know there is some perfection, and perhaps also an infinity of properties of which I am ignorant, are formally or eminently in God, in order that the idea I have of him may be come the most true, clear, and distinct of all the ideas in my mind.

26 —

But perhaps I am something more than I suppose myself to be, and it may be that all those perfections which I attribute to God, in some way exist potentially in me, although they do not yet show themselves, and are not reduced to act. Indeed, I am already conscious that my knowledge is being increased [and perfected] by degrees; and I see nothing to prevent it from thus gradually increasing to infinity, nor any reason why, after such increase and perfection, I should not be able thereby to acquire all the other perfections of the Divine nature; nor, in fine, why the power I possess of acquiring those perfections, if it really now exist in me, should not be sufficient to produce the ideas of them.

distinctly contains more reality than I do. It is clearly, distinctly a Big Idea, which means it *has* to represent something that really exists outside of my mind. In fact, it is clearly a *Biggest* Idea, since it contains all the perfections. Like, I don't have any other idea that explains the idea of God; it's too big to be explained by anything else. I'm not saying I completely, clearly and distinctly *understand* God. That would be fucking crazy. I'm sure there's tons of shit about the Big Guy that I don't understand at all, like why He would allow evil to exist or why bros are His favorite. The important thing is: what I *do* understand clearly and distinctly is the idea of an infinite being with infinite properties. All the ideas of infinite properties are Big Ideas—they have more objective reality than I can cover. So there must be *some* Being out there with enough formal reality to cover the objective reality contained in my idea of God.

WHY DOESN'T OUR HERO NEED TOTAL COMPREHENSION OF GOD TO USE GOD AS A BIG IDEA?

— **26**

Part of me is like, "Aw, dude, don't be so down on yourself. Maybe all these perfections *could* belong to you after all! I mean, you're constantly getting better, learning new things, getting handsomer, and so on. Maybe eventually you'll reach infinity and acquire all these perfections!" After all, I am incredibly handsome. If I could eventually become actually perfect, that means right now I'm *potentially* perfect, which might explain where I got the idea of perfection.

27

Yet, on looking more closely into the matter, I discover that this cannot be; for, in the first place, although it were true that my knowledge daily acquired new degrees of perfection, and although there were potentially in my nature much that was not as yet actually in it, still all these excellences make not the slightest approach to the idea I have of the Deity, in whom there is no perfection merely potentially [but all actually] existent; for it is even an unmistakable token of imperfection in my knowledge, that it is augmented by degrees. Further, although my knowledge increase more and more, nevertheless I am not, therefore, induced to think that it will ever be actually infinite, since it can never reach that point beyond which it shall be incapable of further increase. But I conceive God as actually infinite, so that nothing can be added to his perfection. And, in fine, I readily perceive that the objective being of an idea cannot be produced by a being that is merely potentially existent, which, properly speaking, is nothing, but only by a being existing formally or actually.

28

And, truly, I see nothing in all that I have now said which it is not easy for any one, who shall carefully consider it, to discern by the natural light; but when I allow my attention in some degree to relax, the vision of my mind being obscured, and, as it were, blinded by the images of sensible objects, I do not readily remember the reason why the idea of a being more perfect than myself, must of necessity have proceeded from a being in reality more perfect. On this account I am here desirous to inquire further, whether I, who possess this idea of God, could exist supposing there were no God.

— **27**

No, you know what, fuck that, that's a dumb fucking argument, regardless of how seriously, incredibly handsome I am. Even if I'm constantly improving and even if I have shitloads of potential, there's no way I even come close to the perfections in the idea I have of motherfucking God, for fuckssake. Like, I'm learning a bunch of shit, but that's how you know I'm not perfect yet. I still have shit to learn. According to my idea of God, He is already completely perfect. He's not learning anything because there's nothing else for Him to learn. And I can't learn my way to infinite knowledge—that's like trying to drink infinity drinks. There are always more drinks, that's what makes it infinity. So even if there is some *potential* infinity in me, it can't be the source of enough objective reality for an idea with *actual* infinity. Marv's not gonna stand for that shit at all.

— **28**

Holy shit. Suddenly it's *so obvious* that God exists. Anyone with half a brain who hears about this shit should be able to tell: God has to exist. He can't possibly *not* exist. And all I had to do was fucking pay attention and think clearly about it. Ugh, fuck, but that was so much goddamn work, and I'm so goddamn exhausted after all that shit. I'm worried that tonight I'm going out to celebrate and as soon as I cut loose and relax a little, it'll get harder to see how to get from an *idea* of some perfect thing all the way to the actual *existence* of that thing.

So, let me try something different here, kind of as an insurance policy. Let's say there isn't any God at all. Could I still exist then? I don't think so.

And I ask, from whom could I, in that case, derive my existence? Perhaps from myself, or from my parents, or from some other causes less perfect than God; for anything more perfect, or even equal to God, cannot be thought or imagined.

But if I [were independent of every other existence, and] were myself the author of my being, I should doubt of nothing, I should desire nothing, and, in fine, no perfection would be awanting to me; for I should have bestowed upon myself every perfection of which I possess the idea, and I should thus be God. And it must not be imagined that what is now wanting to me is perhaps of more difficult acquisition than that of which I am already possessed; for, on the contrary, it is quite manifest that it was a matter of much higher difficulty that I, a thinking being, should arise from nothing, than it would be for me to acquire the knowledge of many things of which I am ignorant, and which are merely the accidents of a thinking substance; and certainly, if I possessed of myself the greater perfection of which I have now spoken [in other words, if I were the author of my own existence], I would not at least have denied to myself things that may be more easily obtained [as that infinite variety of knowledge of which I am at present destitute]. I could not, indeed, have denied to myself any property which I perceive is contained in the idea of God, because there is none of these that seems to me to be more difficult to make or acquire; and if there were any that should happen to be more difficult to acquire, they would certainly appear so to me (supposing that I myself were the source of the other things I possess), because I should discover in them a limit to my power.

— **29**

So suppose there were no God. Then my existence must come from somewhere else, somewhere less perfect than God. Obviously this new source of my existence can't be more perfect than God; otherwise, it would just be God. It's not helpful to just say, "Yo there's no God, but there is a totally perfect being." That's just a dumb trick where you rename some shit. So let's say there's no God. Where the fuck did I come from?

— **30**

Maybe I created myself and all my ideas, including the ideas of perfections like infinite substance, infinite knowledge, infinite power, whatever. Since I created those ideas, I have as much formal reality as they have objective reality. But since I have enough reality to create those ideas, I also have enough reality to create those actual perfections. If I could have given myself those perfections, why the fuck wouldn't I? I voluntarily declined? "I could create myself with infinite knowledge, but I like a challenge!" Fuck that. If I could have known everything, I totally would have. On the other hand, if those perfections have more reality than I do, then the idea of those perfections had to come from somewhere else, which would explain why I don't have them.

And it can't be that I managed to create myself from nothing, to fucking pull myself from the Void, but then didn't have the juice to make myself perfect. I could do all that, I could even sneak past Marv, but I couldn't quite give myself these perfections? It sure seems easier to just tack on some additional shit than it is to fucking create myself out of nothing at all in the first place. And if any of those perfections are harder to acquire than existence itself, I feel like I would be able to tell. If I were powerful enough to make some things out of nothing, I would have noticed the limit to my power. I'd be like, "Okay, apparently I can make myself but I can't do it perfectly, because reasons." As it is, I have no idea why I could have the power to create myself without perfections. So wherever the fuck I came from, I didn't create myself.

31

And though I were to suppose that I always was as I now am, I should not, on this ground, escape the force of these reasonings, since it would not follow, even on this supposition, that no author of my existence needed to be sought after. For the whole time of my life may be divided into an infinity of parts, each of which is in no way dependent on any other; and, accordingly, because I was in existence a short time ago, it does not follow that I must now exist, unless in this moment some cause create me anew as it were, that is, conserve me. In truth, it is perfectly clear and evident to all who will attentively consider the nature of duration, that the conservation of a substance, in each moment of its duration, requires the same power and act that would be necessary to create it, supposing it were not yet in existence; so that it is manifestly a dictate of the natural light that conservation and creation differ merely in respect of our mode of thinking [and not in reality].

32

All that is here required, therefore, is that I interrogate myself to discover whether I possess any power by means of which I can bring it about that I, who now am, shall exist a moment afterward: for, since I am merely a thinking thing (or since, at least, the precise question, in the meantime, is only of that part of myself), if such a power resided in me, I should, without doubt, be conscious of it; but I am conscious of no such power, and thereby I manifestly know that I am dependent upon some being different from myself.

33

But perhaps the being upon whom I am dependent is not God, and I have been produced either by my parents, or by some causes less perfect than Deity. This cannot be: for, as I before said, it is perfectly evident that there must at least be as much reality in the cause as in

— **31**

So instead of creating myself at some point, let's say that I have always existed. Now I don't have to worry about my *creation*, but what the fuck is keeping me around? If you chop my life up into like infinitely many little *moments*, there's no reason I have to exist in *one* moment just because I existed in the moment before it. Somehow I had to get into *each moment*, and putting me in each moment is at least as hard as creating me in the *first* moment I existed. So even if I've existed forever, *something* has to be keeping me around.

WHY IS OUR HERO SPENDING TIME ON WHETHER HE CREATED HIMSELF?

— **32**

If I possess the power to sustain myself, I should know about that, right? Like, I shouldn't be *actively sustaining my existence from moment to moment* and not even *be aware* that I have that much power. But I'm clearly not aware of anything like that, so I must lack the power to sustain myself. If I lack the power to sustain myself, I am dependent on some other thing to keep me around all the time. Maybe I don't know who the fuck is running the show, but I know for sure I'm not the one running it.

— **33**

So maybe I come from something else, but that source is less perfect than God. Let's say my source is my dad, that fucker sure as shit isn't perfect. Then my dad must have enough reality to create a thinking being with an idea of God, so my dad must at a *minimum* be himself a thinking

its effect; and accordingly, since I am a thinking thing and possess in myself an idea of God, whatever in the end be the cause of my existence, it must of necessity be admitted that it is likewise a thinking being, and that it possesses in itself the idea and all the perfections I attribute to Deity. Then it may again be inquired whether this cause owes its origin and existence to itself, or to some other cause. For if it be self-existent, it follows, from what I have before laid down, that this cause is God; for, since it possesses the perfection of self-existence, it must likewise, without doubt, have the power of actually possessing every perfection of which it has the idea—in other words, all the perfections I conceive to belong to God. But if it owe its existence to another cause than itself, we demand again, for a similar reason, whether this second cause exists of itself or through some other, until, from stage to stage, we at length arrive at an ultimate cause, which will be God.

34 —

And it is quite manifest that in this matter there can be no infinite regress of causes, seeing that the question raised respects not so much the cause which once produced me, as that by which I am at this present moment conserved.

35 —

Nor can it be supposed that several causes concurred in my production, and that from one I received the idea of one of the perfections I attribute to Deity, and from another the idea of some other, and thus that all those perfections are indeed found somewhere in the universe, but do not all exist together in a single being who is God; for, on the contrary, the unity, the simplicity, or inseparability of all the properties of Deity, is one of the chief perfections I conceive him to possess;

being that has an idea of God. Okay, so question: where the fuck did my dad come from? Since my dad isn't God, he can't be his own source. He has an idea of God, and only God has enough formal reality to cover the idea of God. So I must have someone else to blame for the existence of my asshole father, like my dad's dad. But now, same question: what is the source of *his* dad? Maybe God just *created* my dad, or else maybe I have a granddad, but then where did granddad come from? No matter how many dads you go back, there must be *some dad* with enough reality to *initially create* the idea of God. Eventually, you'll get to some dad that is his own dad, and that dad is God. So even if my parents are the *direct* cause of my existence, somewhere along the line, God had to be at least *indirectly* involved.

— **34**

And it can't be dads all the way down here, like an infinite chain of dads, especially since I wasn't just created, I'm constantly being sustained. No matter how many causes back we go, there has to be *something* at the bottom which not only created me but which is sustaining me right now, something with enough reality to keep the whole goddamn show going on its own. So if I have a single source outside myself, it would have to be as perfect as God.

— **35**

But maybe it's a bunch of different things working together. Like, what if there were a whole bunch of smaller demi-gods, each one with a single perfection? Brad is really big, Tad is really smart, Chad can drink a lot and still be good to drive, and none of them have the same powers. Obviously a bunch of incredibly powerful demi-bros would decide that I'm a worthy creation. So let's imagine I get all these ideas of perfections from The Best Bros Ever, each perfection from a different demi-bro, but then

and the idea of this unity of all the perfections of Deity could certainly
not be put into my mind by any cause from which I did not likewise receive the ideas of all the other perfections; for no power could enable
me to embrace them in an inseparable unity, without at the same time
giving me the knowledge of what they were [and of their existence in a
particular mode].

**LIST THE ALTERNATIVES TO GOD THAT OUR HERO CONSIDERS
AND REJECTS.**

36 —

Finally, with regard to my parents [from whom it appears I sprung],
although all that I believed respecting them be true, it does not, nevertheless, follow that I am conserved by them, or even that I was produced by them, in so far as I am a thinking being. All that, at the most,
they contributed to my origin was the giving of certain dispositions
(modifications) to the matter in which I have hitherto judged that I or
my mind, which is what alone I now consider to be myself, is inclosed;
and thus there can here be no difficulty with respect to them, and it
is absolutely necessary to conclude from this alone that I am, and
possess the idea of a being absolutely perfect, that is, of God, that his
existence is most clearly demonstrated.

37 —

There remains only the inquiry as to the way in which I received this
idea from God; for I have not drawn it from the senses, nor is it even
presented to me unexpectedly, as is usual with the ideas of sensible objects, when these are presented or appear to be presented to
the external organs of the senses; it is not even a pure production or

I mashed those ideas together into one big franken-God idea. If I made all those ideas into one idea, then one of these demi-bros would need the perfection of "unity of all the other perfections," since that's a property my idea of God has. But if this bro had "unity of all the other perfections," he'd just have all the perfections. You can't give me the idea that "all this shit is bundled together" without also giving me the idea "all this shit," whatever it is. So whichever demi-bro gave me the idea of the bundle also gave me the idea of everything in the bundle. Since this bundle contains all the perfections, whoever gave me the idea of this unity would have to have all those perfections anyway. So one of this team of demi-bros is just God. Why the fuck even bother with the others?

36

Now it sure as fuck seems like my parents had something to do with me existing, but even if that's true, that doesn't mean that they sustain me in an ongoing way, or that they're the cause of my true nature as a thinking thing. Seems like all they really did was give me the shape of the body that my mind happens to live in. So there's no way to say my parents must be the *actual* cause of me; there has to be something additional. What additional? Well, I'm out of other options; God has to be the special sauce there. So here's some shit I'm convinced of: I exist, I am a thinking thing, I have the idea of a perfect being, and that perfect being has definitely, clearly been shown to exist.

37

How the fuck did I even get the idea of God from God? It didn't come via the senses; it's not like every once in a while I see God and go, "Oh yeah!" So it's not an idea that came to me from the outside. I also didn't make the idea up, since I can't modify it or change it around in any way, and I never had the power to create it in the first place. Since it didn't come

fiction of my mind, for it is not in my power to take from or add to it; and consequently there but remains the alternative that it is innate, in the same way as is the idea of myself.

38

And, in truth, it is not to be wondered at that God, at my creation, implanted this idea in me, that it might serve, as it were, for the mark of the workman impressed on his work; and it is not also necessary that the mark should be something different from the work itself; but considering only that God is my creator, it is highly probable that he in some way fashioned me after his own image and likeness, and that I perceive this likeness, in which is contained the idea of God, by the same faculty by which I apprehend myself, in other words, when I make myself the object of reflection, I not only find that I am an incomplete, [imperfect] and dependent being, and one who unceasingly aspires after something better and greater than he is; but, at the same time, I am assured likewise that he upon whom I am dependent possesses in himself all the goods after which I aspire [and the ideas of which I find in my mind], and that not merely indefinitely and potentially, but infinitely and actually, and that he is thus God. And the whole force of the argument of which I have here availed myself to establish the existence of God, consists in this, that I perceive I could not possibly be of such a nature as I am, and yet have in my mind the idea of a God, if God did not in reality exist—this same God, I say, whose idea is in my mind—that is, a being who possesses all those lofty perfections, of which the mind may have some slight conception, without, however, being able fully to comprehend them, and who is wholly superior to all defect [and has nothing that marks imperfection]: whence it is sufficiently manifest that he cannot be a deceiver, since it is a dictate of the natural light that all fraud and deception spring from some defect.

from outside of me and I didn't make it up myself, the idea must be an idea I am born with, just like how I'm born with the idea of myself.

— **38**

Looking back it's like, "no shit, God implanted this idea in me." If I'd made a work of art like me, I'd want to sign me too, because I am fucking awesome and I'd want everyone to know. In fact, the work itself might be like a Divine signature, and since He probably fashioned me in His image, I understand Him the same way I understand myself—by reflecting on my own nature. No wonder I am incomplete but improving; God has all the perfections I'm constantly striving for.

Holy shit, I got a surprising amount done today, considering what a shitty, hungover start I had. I showed that if God did not really exist according to the idea that I have of Him, it would be impossible for me to exist and have the idea of Him that I do. Since I exist and have that idea, He must really exist. Also, since my idea of Him represents Him in some way, He must be at least as perfect as I think He is. Finally, since He's that perfect, He cannot be a deceiver, since lying is a bullshit thing only an imperfect dweeb would do.

WHAT DOES OUR HERO THINK HE HAS ACCOMPLISHED IN TODAY'S MEDITATION?

39

But before I examine this with more attention, and pass on to the consideration of other truths that may be evolved out of it, I think it proper to remain here for some time in the contemplation of God himself—that I may ponder at leisure his marvelous attributes—and behold, admire, and adore the beauty of this light so unspeakably great, as far, at least, as the strength of my mind, which is to some degree dazzled by the sight, will permit. For just as we learn by faith that the supreme felicity of another life consists in the contemplation of the Divine majesty alone, so even now we learn from experience that a like meditation, though incomparably less perfect, is the source of the highest satisfaction of which we are susceptible in this life.

— **39**

To celebrate God's infinite goodness, here's the plan: I'mma get real fucked up, safe in the knowledge that since God is infinitely good, He would only allow me to have an infinitely good time.

This is going to be great.

HOW DOES TODAY'S MEDITATION FIT INTO OUR HERO'S LARGER PROJECT?

MEDITATION IV

. . .

Of Truth And Error.

I have been habituated these bygone days to detach my mind from the senses, and I have accurately observed that there is exceedingly little which is known with certainty respecting corporeal objects, that we know much more of the human mind, and still more of God himself. I am thus able now without difficulty to abstract my mind from the contemplation of [sensible or] imaginable objects, and apply it to those which, as disengaged from all matter, are purely intelligible. And certainly the idea I have of the human mind in so far as it is a thinking thing, and not extended in length, breadth, and depth, and participating in none of the properties of body, is incomparably more distinct than the idea of any corporeal object; and when I consider that I doubt, in other words, that I am an incomplete and dependent being, the idea of a complete and independent being, that is to say of God, occurs to my mind with so much clearness and distinctness, and from the fact alone that this idea is found in me, or that I who possess it exist, the conclusions that God exists, and that my own existence, each moment of its continuance, is absolutely dependent upon him, are so manifest, as to lead me to believe it impossible that the human mind can know anything with more clearness and certitude. And now I seem to discover a path that will conduct us from the contemplation

MEDITATION IV

. . .

Of Truth And Error.

— 01

I came here to drink a bunch and see some butts, but instead I've spent all week *ignoring* my senses, because it turns out they tell me almost nothing about what exists. At least I'm sure that I exist, and that I'm a thinking bro, but also that I'm not infinite or perfect. Of course, that makes me think of a being who *is* infinite and perfect, and now, it's super clear to me that God exists and He's infinitely *good* and my existence depends on Him *constantly*. And now see, that's the sort of thing I'm certain about, because it's super clear to me. Now that I know more about God, I *think* I can figure some stuff out about the *other* shit there might be, like physical bodies and other people. Which would be nice, because even though I proved that God is infinitely good, I'm hungover as shit again.

WHAT'S THE GOAL FOR THIS MEDITATION, AND HOW DOES IT FIT INTO THE WHOLE PROJECT?

of the true God, in whom are contained all the treasures of science and wisdom, to the knowledge of the other things in the universe.

02 —

For, in the first place, I discover that it is impossible for him ever to deceive me, for in all fraud and deceit there is a certain imperfection: and although it may seem that the ability to deceive is a mark of subtlety or power, yet the will testifies without doubt of malice and weakness; and such, accordingly, cannot be found in God.

03 —

In the next place, I am conscious that I possess a certain faculty of judging [or discerning truth from error], which I doubtless received from God, along with whatever else is mine; and since it is impossible that he should will to deceive me, it is likewise certain that he has not given me a faculty that will ever lead me into error, provided I use it aright.

04 —

And there would remain no doubt on this head, did it not seem to follow from this, that I can never therefore be deceived; for if all I possess be from God, and if he planted in me no faculty that is deceitful, it seems to follow that I can never fall into error. Accordingly, it is true that when I think only of God (when I look upon myself as coming from God, Fr.), and turn wholly to him, I discover [in myself] no cause of error or falsity: but immediately thereafter, recurring to myself, experience assures me that I am nevertheless subject to innumerable errors. When I come to inquire into the cause of these, I observe that there is not only present to my consciousness a real and

— **02**

Since God is perfect, I know He isn't *lying* to me. Maybe a powerful/smart being would be a better liar than a weak/dumb idiot, but being a liar also makes you a shitty, imperfect dude. God is too perfect to be a shitty dude in any way whatsoever. So there has to be another explanation for why bad things like this hangover happen even though God is perfectly good.

— **03**

I have this ability to pass judgments on stuff. I don't mean just having opinions like "On a scale of 1–10 I give that butt a 'butt out of 10'" or "This is a real tasty brew" or "Yo fuck bananas." When I say "pass judgments" I mean deciding whether I think something is true or false; I can make judgments like "It's true that I exist" or "There is really an external world" or "Oh shit that wasn't Paul Rabil after all." That power has to come from God, since God created me, and since He's not a dick, no power He gives me would fuck me up as long as I use it correctly.

— **04**

Which is weird, because even though my power to make judgments came from God, sometimes I *do* make judgments that are wrong. I'm not wrong a *lot* but I am wrong *sometimes,* which is enough for me to wonder: what the fuck?

Here's an idea: errors are like *absences,* right? It's like "Hey, there's been a mistake, you didn't get enough beer for this party," or else "Yo, something's wrong, there aren't enough people here to drink all this beer." Either way the solution is *more,* not less. So when I fuck up, it's because something is *missing.* There's nothing wrong with any of the powers God gave me, but they're not infinite. So *of course* some correct

positive idea of God, or of a being supremely perfect, but also, so to speak, a certain negative idea of nothing, in other words, of that which is at an infinite distance from every sort of perfection, and that I am, as it were, a mean between God and nothing, or placed in such a way between absolute existence and non-existence, that there is in truth nothing in me to lead me into error, in so far as an absolute being is my creator; but that, on the other hand, as I thus likewise participate in some degree of nothing or of nonbeing, in other words, as I am not myself the supreme Being, and as I am wanting in many perfections, it is not surprising I should fall into error. And I hence discern that error, so far as error is not something real, which depends for its existence on God, but is simply defect; and therefore that, in order to fall into it, it is not necessary God should have given me a faculty expressly for this end, but that my being deceived arises from the circumstance that the power which God has given me of discerning truth from error is not infinite.

05 —

Nevertheless this is not yet quite satisfactory; for error is not a pure negation, [in other words, it is not the simple deficiency or want of some knowledge which is not due], but the privation or want of some knowledge which it would seem I ought to possess. But, on considering the nature of God, it seems impossible that he should have planted in his creature any faculty not perfect in its kind, that is, wanting in some perfection due to it: for if it be true, that in proportion to the skill of the maker the perfection of his work is greater, what thing can have been produced by the supreme Creator of the universe that is not absolutely perfect in all its parts? And assuredly there is no doubt that God could have created me such as that I should never be deceived; it is certain, likewise, that he always wills what is best: is it better, then, that I should be capable of being deceived than that I should not?

judgments are going to be missing; I'm an impressive dude, but I'm not infinitely impressive; *eventually* I have to stop being right all the time.

WHAT'S THE CONFLICT IN 04, AND WHY MIGHT IT BE A PROBLEM FOR THE GOAL OF THIS MEDITATION?

— **05**

Still, absences aren't always a *bad thing*; some things are finite, but that doesn't explain how I make *errors*. If I throw a party with exactly the right beer/person ratio, there could always be more people *and* more beer, but that doesn't mean the party isn't awesome.

So there's shit I don't know, like the names of all the angels or the number of drinks I had last night, but that's fine. A lot of those names are on Wikipedia, and sometimes you just lose count, who cares. The problem is that I pass judgments like "Hey woah that's Paul Rabil" and then I find out that I was wrong like a fucking idiot, and now I look like some kind of new-money asshole who doesn't even know what *world's greatest lacrosse player Paul goddamn Rabil* looks like. It's like, is my grandad even rich? Paul Rabil's face isn't just any old thing to not know, that's some shit I *should* know and *don't*. God can totally create *limited* powers, that's fine, but it's not cool to think He would create powers that are missing

SO ONLY SOME ABSENCES ARE BAD—WHICH ONES?

06 —

Considering this more attentively the first thing that occurs to me
is the reflection that I must not be surprised if I am not always capable of comprehending the reasons why God acts as he does; nor must
I doubt of his existence because I find, perhaps, that there are several
other things besides the present respecting which I understand neither why nor how they were created by him; for, knowing already that
my nature is extremely weak and limited, and that the nature of God,
on the other hand, is immense, incomprehensible, and infinite, I have
no longer any difficulty in discerning that there is an infinity of things
in his power whose causes transcend the grasp of my mind: and this
consideration alone is sufficient to convince me, that the whole class
of final causes is of no avail in physical [or natural] things; for it
appears to me that I cannot, without exposing myself to the charge
of temerity, seek to discover the [impenetrable] ends of Deity.

07 —

It further occurs to me that we must not consider only one creature
apart from the others, if we wish to determine the perfection of the
works of Deity, but generally all his creatures together; for the same
object that might perhaps, with some show of reason, be deemed highly imperfect if it were alone in the world, may for all that be the most
perfect possible, considered as forming part of the whole universe:
and although, as it was my purpose to doubt of everything, I only as
yet know with certainty my own existence and that of God, nevertheless, after having remarked the infinite power of Deity, I cannot
deny that we may have produced many other objects, or at least that

things that *shouldn't be missing*. Like, God is always making the best possible outcome happen, so why the fuck would He make it so that I fuck up sometimes? Maybe it's somehow better that I can be deceived than that I can't? That seems fucked.

— **06**

I don't always know why God does the things He does, and maybe I don't get to start doubting His existence just because His methods seem a little fucked up to me. I'm just some fucking bro, and God is the CEO of everything. So what if there's some shit about Him that I can't wrap my mortal mind around?

WHAT IS AT STAKE? WHAT IF OUR HERO FAILS TO EXPLAIN THE CONFLICT LAID OUT IN 04?

— **07**

Also, maybe some shit that seems broken in isolation is exactly what I need when I take it in context. Someone might be like "Sorry your dad was never around, bro," but when I take it in context it's like "It's totally fine, I always got to go home with my friends after sports games and I never had to go camping, which probably sucks anyway." There are only two things I really understand at all right now: myself and God. Who even knows what crazy context there might be out there to make my mistakes better? Maybe it's like that time where I fucked up real bad by not getting hammered before that party, but it worked out because it meant I was good to smuggle my boys out in my trunk when the cops showed up.

he is able to produce them, so that I may occupy a place in the relation of a part to the great whole of his creatures.

Whereupon, regarding myself more closely, and considering what my errors are (which alone testify to the existence of imperfection in me), I observe that these depend on the concurrence of two causes, viz, the faculty of cognition, which I possess, and that of election or the power of free choice,—in other words, the understanding and the will. For by the understanding alone, I [neither affirm nor deny anything but] merely apprehend (*percipio*) the ideas regarding which I may form a judgment; nor is any error, properly so called, found in it thus accurately taken. And although there are perhaps innumerable objects in the world of which I have no idea in my understanding, it cannot, on that account be said that I am deprived of those ideas [as of something that is due to my nature], but simply that I do not possess them, because, in truth, there is no ground to prove that Deity ought to have endowed me with a larger faculty of cognition than he has actually bestowed upon me; and however skillful a workman I suppose him to be, I have no reason, on that account, to think that it was obligatory on him to give to each of his works all the perfections he is able to bestow upon some. Nor, moreover, can I complain that God has not given me freedom of choice, or a will sufficiently ample and perfect, since, in truth, I am conscious of will so ample and extended as to be superior to all limits. And what appears to me here to be highly remarkable is that, of all the other properties I possess, there is none so great and perfect as that I do not clearly discern it could be still greater and more perfect. For, to take an example, if I consider the faculty of understanding which I possess, I find that it is of very small extent, and greatly limited, and at the same time I form the idea of another faculty of the same nature, much more ample and even infinite, and seeing that I can frame the idea of it, I discover, from this circumstance alone,

So maybe I can find some context that makes sense of my errors, which would be a better explanation than "I dunno, because God?"

— **08**

And before I go blaming God for shit, I should probably figure out *how* I make mistakes. It's probably not as simple as "step one: think a thing, step two: God hates me," right? How *exactly* is it that I go about believing some idea that isn't true? Obviously, my ability to *understand* stuff is important here, because that's how I perceive *any* idea. But no matter how long I sat around and stared at that dude who looked like Paul Rabil, eventually I decided, "Alright, I think that's Paul Rabil." There had to be a moment I made a decision; my free will came into play.

It's only when I activate both of those powers—my power of understanding and my power of free will—that I can believe wrong things. Without the understanding, I don't have any ideas to be wrong *about*; without free will, I'd miss the crucial step where I pull the trigger and go, "Okay, yup, I've decided that's Paul Rabil over there."

So far, nothing to be mad at God about. Like I can't be mad about my limited understanding, because maybe there's tons of shit that I don't have any ideas about, but God doesn't *owe* me those ideas. As long as there's nothing faulty with the ideas He *did* give me, we're still bros. And I definitely can't complain about my free will, because that shit's not limited at all. Like sure, maybe I don't have as many *options* to exercise my free will over as God has; I have to choose between "party over here" and "party over there," while God can party wherever He pleases. But between my two party options, my will itself is totally unlimited; whenever I consider some options I have, I never feel *forced externally* to decide one way or the other. Sometimes one choice is *obviously better* than another, but that's not a *limit* on my freedom; if my drink options are whiskey or rubbing alcohol, I don't have to be like, "Who cares! My will is completely unconstrained! Isn't this fun?!" Freedom includes the ability to choose what I understand to be the right thing; having knowledge

that it pertains to the nature of God. In the same way, if I examine the faculty of memory or imagination, or any other faculty I possess, I find none that is not small and circumscribed, and in God immense [and infinite]. It is the faculty of will only, or freedom of choice, which I experience to be so great that I am unable to conceive the idea of another that shall be more ample and extended; so that it is chiefly my will which leads me to discern that I bear a certain image and similitude of Deity. For although the faculty of will is incomparably greater in God than in myself, as well in respect of the knowledge and power that are conjoined with it, and that render it stronger and more efficacious, as in respect of the object, since in him it extends to a greater number of things, it does not, nevertheless, appear to me greater, considered in itself formally and precisely: for the power of will consists only in this, that we are able to do or not to do the same thing (that is, to affirm or deny, to pursue or shun it), or rather in this alone, that in affirming or denying, pursuing or shunning, what is proposed to us by the understanding, we so act that we are not conscious of being determined to a particular action by any external force. For, to the possession of freedom, it is not necessary that I be alike indifferent toward each of two contraries; but, on the contrary, the more I am inclined toward the one, whether because I clearly know that in it there is the reason of truth and goodness, or because God thus internally disposes my thought, the more freely do I choose and embrace it; and assuredly divine grace and natural knowledge, very far from diminishing liberty, rather augment and fortify it. But the indifference of which I am conscious when I am not impelled to one side rather than to another for want of a reason, is the lowest grade of liberty, and manifests defect or negation of knowledge rather than perfection of will; for if I always clearly knew what was true and good, I should never have any difficulty in determining what judgment I ought to come to, and what choice I ought to make, and I should thus be entirely free without ever being indifferent.

or divine grace helping me out makes my freedom stronger, because it allows me to make better choices. The only time I end up *totally indifferent* between two choices is when I don't know shit about them. If someone asked me, "Hey, which wine should I pair with these vegetables?" it's like, dude, whichever one you can drink the most of? I don't fucking know. Total indifference is freedom at its absolute *lowest*; if I always knew the best thing to do, I would never be indifferent, but I would always be free.

```
N O I T P E C R E P T C N I T S I D D N A R A E L C
N W R N M Y S T E R Y D R I N K S R L L R N V J T Q
E H I I K N O W L E D G E G L Y J A M D V I B K M M
C A M O P E X Y J Y Y D R T Q J M D E X R Z R P Z L
E T A P J C R D N B Q W J M Y X W M Y D T M O S B Q
S I G E L B H U V Y L N J Y G R N G D G I U K V Y N
S F I H D V L A T B G Y B L R V Y N O K R E J M B T
A I N T R B M G D A M V E Y G D A D Q O P R A J N G
R , A N Z V L D W K N V X Y Q K L L N T D T V R X D
Y M T E R X V M W J I L Q L N B A E I Q H N O Z D T
E A I V N N M D T L Z T A I L E O C W E T B I W J V
X L O E L O Z L D G X Y R I R U I D M G J D N M M L
I O N S G H W E Z L R D J T T S L A N E M N K P T N
S N P , W G M R M J T Y , F M N T B C R O R J R K X
T E R T Z O L X D , J N O W Y I E T O I T G V N T P
E Z N A N D R Z N N E R B L C Z I S S D B Q N T D Y
N Y V H M D Y O B R C P R S M V R U S Z Y P D Y G L
C T T W X R D Z A H M P M L E Q L R T E Z M L T G Z
E N T N L T R S A T M N Y R L L L X D K D D J R G V
G V U E J Z T D R J Y T E N I R G R J N T M W N M N
R L B H N T D R V R N A D L Q Y M P M L N R R J N Q
R Q A T U Q N R D M L Y W J Z V J P D M T W N V L B
B Z Q B M G M B T I M R N J R L J L V Q J G D R V D
K N F Q J D X B T Y D R T D R X R Z G K D P Z R L P
Q I W Q R B D Y W G Z N J Y J J D Z M G G Q J Z P R J
```

MIND
BODY
EVIL DEMON
GOD
A BUTT
MATHEMATICS
NECESSARY EXISTENCE
IF BUTTS AREN'T REAL

THEN WHAT'S EVEN
  THE POINT
KNOWLEDGE
CLEAR AND DISTINCT
  PERCEPTION
OH GOD
IMAGINATION
OBJECTIVE REALITY
WHAT IF I'M ALONE

SKEPTICISM
IDEAS
ESSENTIAL NATURE
MYSTERY DRINK
DON'T DRINK AND DRIVE
ILLUSION
RIP CHAD
POUR ONE OUT FOR CHAD

09

From all this I discover, however, that neither the power of willing, which I have received from God, is of itself the source of my errors, for it is exceedingly ample and perfect in its kind; nor even the power of understanding, for as I conceive no object unless by means of the faculty that God bestowed upon me, all that I conceive is doubtless rightly conceived by me, and it is impossible for me to be deceived in it. Whence, then, spring my errors? They arise from this cause alone, that I do not restrain the will, which is of much wider range than the understanding, within the same limits, but extend it even to things I do not understand, and as the will is of itself indifferent to such, it readily falls into error and sin by choosing the false in room of the true, and evil instead of good.

WHAT IS OUR HERO'S EXPLANATION FOR HIS ERRORS?

10

For example, when I lately considered whether aught really existed in the world, and found that because I considered this question, it very manifestly followed that I myself existed, I could not but judge that what I so clearly conceived was true, not that I was forced to this judgment by any external cause, but simply because great clearness of the understanding was succeeded by strong inclination in the will; and I believed this the more freely and spontaneously in proportion as I was less indifferent with respect to it. But now I not only know that I exist, in so far as I am a thinking being, but there is likewise present-

— **09**

So my free will isn't the source of error, because it's fucking perfect and literally unlimited. And my power of understanding isn't the source of error, because if I truly understand something, there's no way for it to be wrong; every idea in my understanding came from not-a-liar God! That time I decided, "Oh shit, that's Paul Rabil!" the problem wasn't that my understanding of Paul Rabil was wrong, it was that I had no understanding of Paul Rabil at all. It's the difference between sticking to a bad plan really well, and going, "There's no plan after all, but fuck it we'll do it live." God doesn't give me bad plans, but I still made the choice to believe that the man I saw was Paul Rabil. I have the power to make choices about things I don't know shit about, and that's when I start fucking things up! Should you drink that strange liquid? I don't fucking know, do whatever you want. But if I'm like "Hey asshole, finish your mystery drink, what's the worst that could happen?" and then my bro Chad is like "Dude I think there was something weird in that mystery drink." Then I'm like "Well, what the fuck did you listen to me for? I didn't know shit about that drink." And then Chad starts vomiting blood and I'm all "Holy shit Chad, do you have any idea how much that carpet costs?! You have to go home man!" And then I have to try to drive him home because suddenly he feels *weird*, and it's this whole... thing. Fuck.

— **10**

I'm at least doing better, though. For example, I seem to be handling this crazy week well: I asked whether I existed, and I decided that even asking the question is proof that yes, obviously I exist. That pretty much locked me into the judgment "it is true that I exist." I could have insisted, "But what if I *don't* exist?!" but that would just make me a stubborn asshole. The more clear and distinct my understanding became, the less indifferent I was. The less indifferent I was, the more I wanted to believe: I exist.

Now I'm trying to decide if this sweet body I perceive is real or not, and I have no idea one way or the other. Maybe my body is essential to my

ed to my mind a certain idea of corporeal nature; hence I am in doubt as to whether the thinking nature which is in me, or rather which I myself am, is different from that corporeal nature, or whether both are merely one and the same thing, and I here suppose that I am as yet ignorant of any reason that would determine me to adopt the one belief in preference to the other; whence it happens that it is a matter of perfect indifference to me which of the two suppositions I affirm or deny, or whether I form any judgment at all in the matter.

11 —

This indifference, moreover, extends not only to things of which the understanding has no knowledge at all, but in general also to all those which it does not discover with perfect clearness at the moment the will is deliberating upon them; for, however probable the conjectures may be that dispose me to form a judgment in a particular matter, the simple knowledge that these are merely conjectures, and not certain and indubitable reasons, is sufficient to lead me to form one that is directly the opposite. Of this I lately had abundant experience, when I laid aside as false all that I had before held for true, on the single ground that I could in some degree doubt of it.

12 —

But if I abstain from judging of a thing when I do not conceive it with sufficient clearness and distinctness, it is plain that I act rightly, and am not deceived; but if I resolve to deny or affirm, I then do not make a right use of my free will; and if I affirm what is false, it is evident that I am deceived; moreover, even although I judge according to truth, I stumble upon it by chance, and do not therefore escape the imputation of a wrong use of my freedom; for it is a dictate of the natural light, that the knowledge of the understanding ought always to precede the determination of the will. And it is this wrong use of the freedom of the will in which is found the privation that constitutes the form of

very existence, and maybe I don't need it even a little bit. I could go either way. Since I could go either way, I shouldn't decide at all. I owe Chad that much, at least.

WHEN DOES OUR HERO THINK IT'S OKAY TO MAKE A JUDGMENT?

- ## 11
There's *tons* of shit I'm indifferent about, it isn't just mystery drinks and the existence of my body. I'm indifferent about *any* choice where there isn't clearly and distinctly a correct option. I don't give a shit what's *probably* correct; that's what got me in this mess in the first place. There's *probably* an external world, right? But *maybe* not. See, and as soon as I admit that it's possible there's *not* an external world, it's like, "Oh shit, maybe despite all this evidence there isn't an external world after all, oh fuck oh fuck."

- ## 12
If I don't want to be wrong about shit, I have to hold off on passing judgment unless I can be *sure* I'm making the correct choice. There doesn't need to be some evil demon doing some complicated deception shit for me to fuck up from time to time; I fuck things completely up on my own every time I say, "Sure, yeah, that's true," to something that I don't totally understand. It sucks when I end up being wrong about that shit, but it's still a fuck up when I get lucky and it turns out I'm right by accident, since as far as I knew it still *could* have gone the other way. I should understand things before I judge whether they're true or not; errors happen when I misuse my free will. So if I'm trying to decide whose fault it is when I fuck

error. Privation, I say, is found in the act, in so far as it proceeds from myself, but it does not exist in the faculty which I received from God, nor even in the act, in so far as it depends on him.

13 —

For I have assuredly no reason to complain that God has not given me a greater power of intelligence or more perfect natural light than he has actually bestowed, since it is of the nature of a finite understanding not to comprehend many things, and of the nature of a created understanding to be finite; on the contrary, I have every reason to render thanks to God, who owed me nothing, for having given me all the perfections I possess, and I should be far from thinking that he has unjustly deprived me of, or kept back, the other perfections which he has not bestowed upon me.

14 —

I have no reason, moreover, to complain because he has given me a will more ample than my understanding, since, as the will consists only of a single element, and that indivisible, it would appear that this faculty is of such a nature that nothing could be taken from it [without destroying it]; and certainly, the more extensive it is, the more cause I have to thank the goodness of him who bestowed it upon me.

15 —

And, finally, I ought not also to complain that God concurs with me in forming the acts of this will, or the judgments in which I am deceived, because those acts are wholly true and good, in so far as they depend on God; and the ability to form them is a higher degree of perfection in my nature than the want of it would be. With regard to privation, in which alone consists the formal reason of error and sin, this does not require the concurrence of Deity, because it is not a thing [or existence], and if it be referred to God as to its cause, it ought not to be

up, this makes it pretty clear: it is definitely my own stupid-goddamn-idiot fault when I *misuse* my will; it is not a problem with my God-given free will itself.

— **13**

I can't complain that God should have made me smarter than I am; I don't understand all His reasons. Who knows why He didn't give me a greater power of understanding? As far as I can tell, He doesn't owe me anything so I should really just be thankful for all the great powers He did give me instead of whining like a baby about what else I wish I could do.

— **14**

Also, I can't complain that He gave me a will that can go beyond my understanding; for starters, there's no way to reduce or scale the will back at all. It's a very simple power: either I can freely choose, or I can't. Besides, even if God *could* weaken it, am I really going to be the asshole who complains that God has given me *too much freedom?*

— **15**

Finally, I can't complain that somehow God shares responsibility for my shitty fuckups. Sure, He gave me the power to make choices, but that's definitely a good thing. I'm way better, more perfect, than I would be without that power. God contributes only goodness to my decisions. If some of my decisions are fuck-ups, that part must come from me. It's fine if I don't know everything; some gaps in my knowledge are fine. A knowledge-gap is only a *bad* thing if I'm missing something and it *should be there*. Like if I'm *deprived* of something that I *need*, that's

called privation, but negation [according to the signification of these words in the schools]. For in truth it is no imperfection in Deity that he has accorded to me the power of giving or withholding my assent from certain things of which he has not put a clear and distinct knowledge in my understanding; but it is doubtless an imperfection in me that I do not use my freedom aright, and readily give my judgment on matters which I only obscurely and confusedly conceive. I perceive, nevertheless, that it was easy for Deity so to have constituted me as that I should never be deceived, although I still remained free and possessed of a limited knowledge, *viz.*, by implanting in my understanding a clear and distinct knowledge of all the objects respecting which I should ever have to deliberate; or simply by so deeply engraving on my memory the resolution to judge of nothing without previously possessing a clear and distinct conception of it, that I should never forget it. And I easily understand that, in so far as I consider myself as a single whole, without reference to any other being in the universe, I should have been much more perfect than I now am, had Deity created me superior to error; but I cannot therefore deny that it is not somehow a greater perfection in the universe, that certain of its parts are not exempt from defect, as others are, than if they were all perfectly alike. And I have no right to complain because God, who placed me in the world, was not willing that I should sustain that character which of all others is the chief and most perfect.

16 —

I have even good reason to remain satisfied on the ground that, if he has not given me the perfection of being superior to error by the first means I have pointed out above, which depends on a clear and evident knowledge of all the matters regarding which I can deliberate, he has at least left in my power the other means, which is, firmly to retain the

a *privation*. Since privations are absences, they don't get any existence from God. If God decided to leave something out, it must be because I don't need to know it, so it's not a privation. It's true that I don't know the names of all the angels, but if God left that out then it's definitely not going to be on the final.

Anyway, what I'm trying to say is that it's not a problem that God allows me to pass judgment on shit I don't understand very well. It's not like He specifically *wants* me to do that: He just happened to give me the power to pass judgment on whatever I want, *including* shit I don't understand. The only imperfection at all here is that instead of using my power correctly, I run around judging all kinds of shit that isn't clear or distinct.

Maybe there are a couple of ways He could have prevented me from making dumbass choices. He could have given me a clear and distinct understanding of everything I would ever have to make a choice about, or He could have given me even stronger instincts against choosing things that aren't clear and distinct. He could have made choices I don't understand completely as scary as standing at the edge of a cliff or, I don't know, what are people afraid of? Heights? And maybe if it were impossible for me to make mistakes, I personally would be more perfect. No shit, right? But that doesn't mean that the universe as a *whole* would be better. After all, if *everything* were perfect, wouldn't that be kind of boring? Maybe? I don't know, but if there's some way that the universe overall is improved, I can't complain that God didn't make *me* one of the perfect parts—after all, it's His universe. He gets to decide whatever the fuck He wants about it.

— **16**

Besides, if God were going to create me so that it's *impossible* for me to fuck up, He would have to give me clear and distinct knowledge of literally everything I think about. And even though He made it possible for me to fuck up, He also made it possible for me to *not* fuck up. There's all the potential for error, but I seem to be doing pretty well today, right? All I

resolution never to judge where the truth is not clearly known to me: for, although I am conscious of the weakness of not being able to keep my mind continually fixed on the same thought, I can nevertheless, by attentive and oft-repeated meditation, impress it so strongly on my memory that I shall never fail to recollect it as often as I require it, and I can acquire in this way the habitude of not erring.

17 —

And since it is in being superior to error that the highest and chief perfection of man consists, I deem that I have not gained little by this day's meditation, in having discovered the source of error and falsity. And certainly this can be no other than what I have now explained: for as often as I so restrain my will within the limits of my knowledge, that it forms no judgment except regarding objects which are clearly and distinctly represented to it by the understanding, I can never be deceived; because every clear and distinct conception is doubtless something, and as such cannot owe its origin to nothing, but must of necessity have God for its author— God, I say, who, as supremely perfect, cannot, without a contradiction, be the cause of any error; and consequently it is necessary to conclude that every such conception [or judgment] is true. Nor have I merely learned to-day what I must avoid to escape error, but also what I must do to arrive at the knowledge of truth; for I will assuredly reach truth if I only fix my attention sufficiently on all the things I conceive perfectly, and separate these from others which I conceive more confusedly and obscurely; to which for the future I shall give diligent heed.

need to do is withhold judgment about things I don't understand completely. If that's too hard for me to focus on all the time, I should find a way to remind myself a whole bunch, like maybe leaving notes that say "DON'T FUCK UP" around my place or putting a rubber band between all these LiveStrong bracelets on my wrist or some shit. God has totally given me the tools to avoid error if I want it badly enough, all I have to do is make a habit of *not doing idiot things.*

— **17**

Since avoiding error can help me be the very best I can be, obviously today has been just a huge day. As long as I don't use my will to make decisions about shit that I don't completely understand or form judgments about shit that isn't clear and distinct, it's actually *impossible* for me to be deceived or otherwise fuck shit up. Clear and distinct conceptions are the ideas I can be sure actually exist, which means they have to come from God in some sense, so *those* don't deceive me since, reminder, God is perfect and can't deceive me. So clear and distinct knowledge I can be sure about.

Not only have I learned how *not to fuck up*, I've also figured out how to *know more things*. I'm *really* sure that perfect understanding, clear and distinct perception, is the way to learn shit—I can just ignore what's confused or unclear and focus on the good stuff.

You know what seems clear and distinct? I need to celebrate this big fucking win. So here's the plan: I'mma get fucked up, secure in the knowledge that as long as I don't make any bad decisions, nothing can go wrong.

MEDITATION V

. . .

Of The Essence of Material Things;
And, Again, of God; That He Exists.

01 —

Several other questions remain for consideration respecting the attributes of God and my own nature or mind. I will, however, on some
other occasion perhaps resume the investigation of these. Meanwhile,
as I have discovered what must be done and what avoided to arrive at
the knowledge of truth, what I have chiefly to do is to essay to emerge
from the state of doubt in which I have for some time been, and to
discover whether anything can be known with certainty regarding
material objects.

02 —

But before considering whether such objects as I conceive exist
without me, I must examine their ideas in so far as these are to be
found in my consciousness, and discover which of them are distinct
and which confused.

03 —

In the first place, I distinctly imagine that quantity which the philoso-
phers commonly call continuous, or the extension in length, breadth,

MEDITATION V

. . .

Of The Essence of Material Things;
And, Again, of God; That He Exists.

— **01**

Yesterday, I finally figured out that the only way *I can know anything at all* is by sticking to my clear and distinct ideas, but fuck me if I'm not hungover again. I really need to get to the bottom of this whole "God" business because I'm sick of this shit. I've already spent four days just moping around and doubting everything like an asshole, sooner or later I better fucking figure out whether I actually have any clear and distinct ideas about material shit, so I don't have to leave Spring Break as a god-damn hungover pit of despair.

— **02**

So I have a bunch of ideas in my mind, and they're supposed to be pictures of things existing *outside* my mind, in some sort of external physical world. But do these ideas *actually* represent anything that exists outside my mind? Well, I know that my *clear and distinct ideas* are the key to figuring shit out, so first I'll separate my ideas into "clear and distinct ideas" and "ideas that can get the fuck outta here."

— **03**

One really clear and distinct idea I have is that there *could* be forms and shapes that are extended in space, and those things would be *totally*

and depth that is in this quantity, or rather in the object to which it is attributed. Further, I can enumerate in it many diverse parts, and attribute to each of these all sorts of sizes, figures, situations, and local motions; and, in fine, I can assign to each of these motions all degrees of duration.

04 —

And I not only distinctly know these things when I thus consider them in general; but besides, by a little attention, I discover innumerable particulars respecting figures, numbers, motion, and the like, which are so evidently true, and so accordant with my nature, that when I now discover them I do not so much appear to learn anything new, as to call to remembrance what I before knew, or for the first time to remark what was before in my mind, but to which I had not hitherto directed my attention.

05 —

And what I here find of most importance is, that I discover in my mind innumerable ideas of certain objects, which cannot be esteemed pure negations, although perhaps they possess no reality beyond my thought, and which are not framed by me though it may be in my power to think, or not to think them, but possess true and immutable natures of their own. As, for example, when I imagine a triangle, although there is not perhaps and never was in any place in the universe apart from my thought one such figure, it remains true nevertheless that this figure possesses a certain determinate nature, form, or essence, which is immutable and eternal, and not framed by me, nor in any degree dependent on my thought; as appears from the circumstance, that diverse properties of the triangle may be demonstrated,

continuous rather than made up of like glued-together smaller parts. So, like, it seems like we've got a keg in the sand over there, and it's supposed to be filled with beer. But it's not like the 30-rack we've got in the cooler over here, where we've got 30 *discrete cans* of beer. With a 30-rack, each time you finish a beer you have to open the next one. With a keg, each sip just flows naturally into the next one. The finish line for one sip and the start line for the next one are the *same line*, so I can drink *continuously* without ever having to stop and count drinks.

— **04**

So it's clear and distinct that "continuous" is a *way shit can be*, but I also have clear and distinct ideas about *particular kinds* of things that are continuous, things like circles and kegs and being rad. I also have clear and distinct ideas about math and stuff, and about motion, including movement in any particular direction, and so on. All that shit makes *so much* goddamn sense to me! It honestly feels less like I'm learning anything and more like I'm remembering how it's always been. It's like even though I didn't know, I totally *actually* knew all along.

— **05**

Some of my ideas are definitely made up and I can say whatever I want about them, like that time I doodled Squats Dad in all my geometry class notes because that class was boring as fuck. Was he a squat rack who was also my father, or was he a dad who only did squats? Who gives a fuck? I can change whatever I want about Squats Dad, because he only exists in my mind. I invented him.

On the other hand, I have some ideas that I *can't* change around, no matter how hard I try. Next to Squats Dad I had a bunch of notes about triangles, and whenever I imagine a triangle, it has some properties that I can't change or get rid of. Triangles *have to* have 180 degrees inside them. If I try to imagine a triangle with only 170 degrees inside, I literally just fail. The closest I can get is imagining some weird non-triangle, like

viz, that its three angles are equal to two right, that its greatest side is subtended by its greatest angle, and the like, which, whether I will or not, I now clearly discern to belong to it, although before I did not at all think of them, when, for the first time, I imagined a triangle, and which accordingly cannot be said to have been invented by me.

06 —

Nor is it a valid objection to allege, that perhaps this idea of a triangle came into my mind by the medium of the senses, through my having. seen bodies of a triangular figure; for I am able to form in thought an innumerable variety of figures with regard to which it cannot be supposed that they were ever objects of sense, and I can nevertheless demonstrate diverse properties of their nature no less than of the triangle, all of which are assuredly true since I clearly conceive them: and they are therefore something, and not mere negations; for it is highly evident that all that is true is something, [truth being identical with existence]; and I have already fully shown the truth of the principle, that whatever is clearly and distinctly known is true. And although this had not been demonstrated, yet the nature of my mind is such as to compel me to assert to what I clearly conceive while I so conceive it; and I recollect that even when I still strongly adhered to the objects of sense, I reckoned among the number of the most certain truths those I clearly conceived relating to figures, numbers, and other matters that pertain to arithmetic and geometry, and in general to the pure mathematics.

07 —

But now if because I can draw from my thought the idea of an object, it follows that all I clearly and distinctly apprehend to pertain to this object, does in truth belong to it, may I not from this derive an argu-

someone bent a coat hanger out of shape. That's not a triangle, it's just a shitty coat hanger. No matter how I try to manipulate my idea of triangles, the 180-degree thing is true; somehow triangles have facts about them that exist independently of my mind.

— **06**

Maybe the idea of a triangle isn't some mystical, far-out idea; maybe I just took my idea of a triangle from the ideas of mundane triangular shit like sailboat sails and paper footballs and Doritos, instead of figuring it out on my own. But I could just as easily prove shit about a shape I've *definitely* never seen before, like a shape with a hundred sides instead of three. I remember learning a formula for how many degrees the angles of a shape add up to, and it worked no matter how many sides a shape had. So even though I've never, ever seen anything with 100 sides, I am clearly, distinctly aware that the angles add up to a certain number. Because I am clearly, distinctly aware of that fact, the fact must be true, even if it doesn't apply to anything *physical*. And since it's a true fact, it has *some* reality, rather than no reality. I have to accept what seems clear and distinct, right? Like, if something seems obviously, clearly true, and I understand *why* it has to be true, and I can see each step on the *way* to knowing that it's true, that's just some shit I have to believe. How the fuck do I look at all that clarity and certainty and go, "Okay, but still?!" I've reached the bottom. I can't dig any further, I'll just break my shovel. Even before today, mathematical ideas and ideas about abstract objects seemed like some of the most obvious and definitely true things I've ever thought about, and this just confirms it.

— **07**

So if I have an idea of some Thing, and I clearly, distinctly perceive that this Thing has some Property, then it must be true that this Thing does in fact have that Property. The idea of a Supremely Perfect Being is at least

ment for the existence of God? It is certain that I no less find the idea of a God in my consciousness, that is the idea of a being supremely perfect, than that of any figure or number whatever: and I know with not less clearness and distinctness that an [actual and] eternal existence pertains to his nature than that all which is demonstrable of any figure or number really belongs to the nature of that figure or number; and, therefore, although all the conclusions of the preceding Meditations were false, the existence of God would pass with me for a truth at least as certain as I ever judged any truth of mathematics to be.

08 —

Indeed such a doctrine may at first sight appear to contain more sophistry than truth. For, as I have been accustomed in every other matter to distinguish between existence and essence, I easily believe that the existence can be separated from the essence of God, and that thus God may be conceived as not actually existing. But, nevertheless, when I think of it more attentively, it appears that the existence can no more be separated from the essence of God, than the idea of a mountain from that of a valley, or the equality of its three angles to two right angles, from the essence of a [rectilinear] triangle; so that it is not less impossible to conceive a God, that is, a being supremely perfect, to whom existence is awanting, or who is devoid of a certain perfection, than to conceive a mountain without a valley.

WHY IS IT SIGNIFICANT THAT TRIANGLES HAVE SOME FIXED PROPERTIES?

---

as clear and distinct as any number or shape, and I think I'm about to find *another* proof that God exists. Honestly at this point I'm just showing off. Go big or go home, baby.

Just like I know from the clear, distinct idea of a triangle that a triangle has 180 degrees, I know from the clear, distinct idea of God that He exists, because the clear, distinct idea of a Supremely Perfect Being tells me that He has property of eternal existence. That property is *at least* as clear to me as all the math bullshit I'm sure about; if I want to say that God isn't real, I'd also have to throw math out the window. This is true even if I'm wrong about all the *other* ways I know God exists, like the "Biggest Idea" thing.

— **08**

Maybe it seems weird to say that God has a property, just because I can conceive of Him with that property. Why can't I just conceive of a God that doesn't exist? Couldn't there just be an idea of something that has all the same properties as God, minus the property of existence? Let's call him God-minus.™ Isn't that easy? Could it be that instead I have a clear, distinct idea of God-minus™?

Well, so, some ideas just *always go together*. Sometimes things (and the ideas of those things) *have to show up in pairs*. You can't have an idea of a beach without *also* having the idea of the shore; the two just go hand in hand. They *always* party in pairs. It's like they're two sides of the same coin. In fact, if a beach *tried* to show up to a party without a shore, Marv would just shake his head and be like, "Nope. You can't come in here alone. Where the fuck is the waterline chick you're on the list with?"

Now let's say there's a Supremely Perfect Partier. His name is—I don't know, just picking out of a hat here—*God*. What would He have to be like? Well, for one thing, if He's a Supremely Perfect Partier, He sure as shit better be *at the fucking party*. You can try to imagine a guy with all the same properties as the Supremely Perfect Partier, except he's at home having a quiet night in, but we *can't call that guy the ultimate*

HOW ARE "PARTIER" AND "BEING" PARALLEL HERE?

09

But though, in truth, I cannot conceive a God unless as existing, any more than I can a mountain without a valley, yet, just as it does not follow that there is any mountain in the world merely because I conceive a mountain with a valley, so likewise, though I conceive God as existing, it does not seem to follow on that account that God exists; for my thought imposes no necessity on things; and as I may imagine a winged horse, though there be none such, so I could perhaps attribute existence to God, though no God existed.

WHY CAN'T WE JUST MAKE UP "NECESSARILY EXISTING BEINGS" OTHER THAN GOD?

10

But the cases are not analogous, and a fallacy lurks under the semblance of this objection: for because I cannot conceive a mountain without a valley, it does not follow that there is any mountain or valley in existence, but simply that the mountain or valley, whether they do or do not exist, are inseparable from each other; whereas, on the other hand, because I cannot conceive God unless as existing, it follows that existence is inseparable from him, and therefore that he really exists: not that this is brought about by my thought, or that it imposes any necessity on things, but, on the contrary, the necessity which lies in the thing itself, that is, the necessity of the existence of God, deter-

partier. Maybe that's God's introvert twin-brother Carl or some shit, I don't know, but he's definitely different from God, because the idea of a Supremely Perfect Partier necessarily includes the idea of Being At The Party. So God-minus™ *isn't* a Supremely Perfect Partier. He isn't a partier at all, since he *doesn't party.*

— **09**

Alright, so maybe I can't picture a beach without a coastline, or a Supremely Perfect Being who doesn't exist. That doesn't mean there are beaches and coastlines *at every party,* it just means that they always travel together, so if I'm missing one I'm missing the other. And just because I *conceive* of a Supremely Perfect Being, that's supposed to be enough? He definitely exists just because I *think of Him that way*? Look, I'm picturing an Ultimate Party Pegasus! Obviously this horse has wings and also has to be at the party! Who gives a fuck? That doesn't mean there really is a flying horse at the party, right? My thoughts don't *force shit to exist.* Imagine if every time I thought of something, that thing existed. What a goddamn nightmare, right? You'd need a snorkel and a chainsaw to get through all those butts. Maybe I'm making the same mistake about God; maybe I'm pretending my thoughts *force Him to exist.*

— **10**

Oh, but here's why *that* objection doesn't work. There's no reason every party *needs* a beach and a shoreline; we just know that if one of them shows up, they both show up. They don't have to exist, they just have to exist *together.* But the thing we know about the Supremely Perfect Partier is that he *can't not party.* He's not linked necessarily to other party guests, He's linked necessarily to *the party itself.* It's not that I imagine Him, and so He must party; it's that He must party, so I can't imagine Him any other way. A Supremely Perfect Partier that doesn't party *isn't an Supremely Perfect Partier*; he's maybe a pretty good partier but nothing legendary or anything. On the other hand, slap some

mines me to think in this way: for it is not in my power to conceive a God without existence, that is, a being supremely perfect, and yet devoid of an absolute perfection, as I am free to imagine a horse with or without wings.

11 —

Nor must it be alleged here as an objection, that it is in truth necessary to admit that God exists, after having supposed him to possess all perfections, since existence is one of them, but that my original supposition was not necessary; just as it is not necessary to think that all quadrilateral figures can be inscribed in the circle, since, if I supposed this, I should be constrained to admit that the rhombus, being a figure of four sides, can be therein inscribed, which, however, is manifestly false. This objection is, I say, incompetent; for although it may not be necessary that I shall at any time entertain the notion of Deity, yet each time I happen to think of a first and sovereign being, and to draw, so to speak, the idea of him from the storehouse of the mind, I am necessitated to attribute to him all kinds of perfections, though I may not then enumerate them all, nor think of each of them in particular. And this necessity is sufficient, as soon as I discover that existence is a perfection, to cause me to infer the existence of this first and sovereign being; just as it is not necessary that I should ever imagine any triangle, but whenever I am desirous of considering a rectilinear figure composed of only three angles, it is absolutely necessary to attribute those properties to it from which it is correctly inferred that its three angles are not greater than two right angles, although perhaps I may not then advert to this relation in particular. But when I consider what figures are capable of being inscribed in the circle, it is by no means necessary to hold that all quadrilateral figures are of this number; on the contrary, I cannot even imagine such to be the case, so long as I

wings on a horse and take him to a party, or don't, I don't give a shit. Nothing about a winged horse says "Winged horses must party all the time;" a party with winged horses is a dope-ass party, yes, but even if there aren't any horses I'm still like, "Well, okay, party on anyways, I guess." There's nothing clear and distinct about an Ultimate Party Horse, but I *do* have a clear and distinct idea of a Supremely Perfect Being.

— **11**

Am I sure I'm not just *defining* God into existence? If we just *define* things so that God has all the perfections, then *obviously* God is at the party: partying is a perfection. But who says God has all the perfections? Why do we have to define it that way? Hah, maybe it's like when that shitty kid in my English class was all, "Let's define 'your birthday party' as 'that night everyone got laid.' I was at that party, so I got laid!" It's like, hold on a second, nerdballs, we know you were at that party, and we also know you didn't get laid. You can't just *define* your way out of your teenage virginity. Maybe it's the same with this God situation: if you *assume* the Supremely Perfect Partier has all the perfections, then sure, God exists, but how do we know that first part is true? Isn't that what we're trying to show? Maybe He's missing some perfections like, for instance, *existence*.

No, that's not the problem: there's no way to *not* assume that God has all the perfections. I guess I could just *never, ever think of God*, but that ship has sailed. Now that I *am* thinking of Him, I'm sort of forced to admit that He'd have all the perfections. Saying He's missing existence is like saying, "Imagine a Supremely Perfect Being that isn't all the way perfect," which doesn't make sense, right? That's gibberish. When I consider my birthday party, there's nothing clear and distinct about the idea that *everyone* got laid; I throw pretty good parties, some might say the literal best parties, but even I can't *absolutely guarantee* that mathsack over there got his dick touched. On the other hand, the clear and distinct idea I have of a perfect being definitely includes *all the perfections*. So there's a *huge* difference between God and my birthday party.

shall be unwilling to accept in thought aught that I do not clearly and distinctly conceive; and consequently there is a vast difference between false suppositions, as is the one in question, and the true ideas that were born with me, the first and chief of which is the idea of God. For indeed I discern on many grounds that this idea is not factitious depending simply on my thought, but that it is the representation of a true and immutable nature: in the first place because I can conceive no other being, except God, to whose essence existence [necessarily] pertains; in the second, because it is impossible to conceive two or more gods of this kind; and it being supposed that one such God exists, I clearly see that he must have existed from all eternity, and will exist to all eternity; and finally, because I apprehend many other properties in God, none of which I can either diminish or change.

12 —

But, indeed, whatever mode of probation I in the end adopt, it always returns to this, that it is only the things I clearly and distinctly conceive which have the power of completely persuading me. And although, of the objects I conceive in this manner, some, indeed, are obvious to every one, while others are only discovered after close and careful investigation; nevertheless after they are once discovered, the latter are not esteemed less certain than the former. Thus, for example, to take the case of a right-angled triangle, although it is not so manifest at first that the square of the base is equal to the squares of the other two sides, as that the base is opposite to the greatest angle; nevertheless, after it is once apprehended, we are as firmly persuaded of the truth of the former as of the latter. And, with respect to God if I were not pre-occupied by prejudices, and my thought beset on all sides by the continual presence of the images of sensible objects, I should know nothing sooner or more easily then the fact of his being. For is there any truth more clear than the existence of a Supreme Being, or of God, seeing it is to his essence alone that [necessary and eternal] existence pertains?

Honestly, there are a lot of reasons to think I didn't just make up this idea of God that I have: for one, it's impossible to clearly, distinctly conceive of *another* being who is necessarily linked to existence the way God is. If I were making this up, seems like it would be easy to make up another necessarily-existing being just as easily as the first one, but not only can I not make up a new necessarily-existing being, I can't even conceive of two copies of this exact one existing simultaneously. Given that one such being, God, exists, I have to admit He has partied forever, and will keep on partying for eternity; I can't change any of his properties at all. They're unchangeable, just like the 180-triangle thing.

— **12**

This keeps coming back to the fact that only clear and distinct ideas are persuasive. "Clear and distinct" doesn't necessarily mean "*obvious.*" Sometimes I have to do a ton of thinking about an idea before it becomes clear and distinct, like all that math homework I had to do instead of spitting game and hitting the gym. No matter how hard it is to clarify an idea for myself, though, once I do understand an idea clearly and distinctly, that idea is *super* fucking persuasive. When I learned that the longest side of a triangle is across from the biggest angle, I was like, "Yeah, that's pretty much what I figured, cool." But when I saw the proof for the Pythagorean Theorem I was like "Holy shit, really? For every single right triangle? Fuck me that is mind-blowing, and also useful for this very specific class where this asshole keeps giving me quizzes about right triangles because his dad couldn't get him a job at a bank." Like at first, the proof kinda blew my mind, but once I took some time to wrap my head around it, the idea was just as clear and distinct to me as the first thing about long sides and big angles. Once I get past my stupid anti-God prejudices and block out sensory information for like one fucking

13 —

And although the right conception of this truth has cost me much close thinking, nevertheless at present I feel not only as assured of it as of what I deem most certain, but I remark further that the certitude of all other truths is so absolutely dependent on it that without this knowledge it is impossible ever to know anything perfectly.

14 —

For although I am of such a nature as to be unable, while I possess a very clear and distinct apprehension of a matter, to resist the conviction of its truth, yet because my constitution is also such as to incapacitate me from keeping my mind continually fixed on the same object, and as I frequently recollect a past judgment without at the same time being able to recall the grounds of it, it may happen meanwhile that other reasons are presented to me which would readily cause me to change my opinion, if I did not know that God existed; and thus I should possess no true and certain knowledge, but merely vague and vacillating opinions. Thus, for example, when I consider the nature of the [rectilinear] triangle, it most clearly appears to me, who have been instructed in the principles of geometry, that its three angles are equal to two right angles, and I find it impossible to believe otherwise, while I apply my mind to the demonstration; but as soon as I cease from attending to the process of proof, although I still remember that I had a clear comprehension of it, yet I may readily come to doubt of the truth demonstrated, if I do not know that there is a God: for I may

second, God's existence is the easiest and most obvious thing in the world to know. For fuckssake, is there anything more obvious than the fact that a God who *necessarily* exists also *actually* exists?

— **13**

So even though it took me until fucking day four of The Weirdest Spring Break Ever to understand that God has the property of existence, it is literally one of the things I am absolutely most certain about; nothing is *more* certain to me than that God exists, not even my *own* existence. In fact, if I can't be sure that God exists, then literally everything else I've ever believed is totally out the window. Without God, I'm stuck not knowing anything ever.

— **14**

That seems extreme. *Everything* else is out the window? Well, obviously I have to believe whatever is clear and distinct to me, right? But that's too much shit to remember all at once. I can't be reciting that in my head and trying to order drinks at a bar and scoping out butts AND honoring Chad's memory all at once. It's easy to prove that there are 180 degrees in a triangle, and for a while after reviewing the proof, I understand *why* there are 180 degrees. It's impossible to doubt. But I go and get lunch, race boats with my bros, stop focusing on boring-ass triangles for a bit. Suddenly my bro pokes his head into the room and goes, "Hey bro, how many degrees in a triangle? 270?" and I'm like, "Nah bro, it's 180." And he says, "Bro are you sure?" and suddenly I'm like, "Yyyyyyyesss? Yes. Yes? You can know that because... fuck, bro, I forget the proof, but I definitely remember it being 180." Without knowing whether God existed, I have to wonder if maybe I could still fuck things up, even though I was super clear on them at one point. So now even though I've seen a proof I'm like, "Right? Is it 180? I'm... pretty sure? Fuck, maybe I'm wrong about the proof, too." And then I remember every single time ever that I was *pretty*

persuade myself that I have been so constituted by nature as to be sometimes deceived, even in matters which I think I apprehend with the greatest evidence and certitude, especially when I recollect that I frequently considered many things to be true and certain which other reasons afterward constrained me to reckon as wholly false.

15 —

But after I have discovered that God exists, seeing I also at the same time observed that all things depend on him, and that he is no deceiver, and thence inferred that all which I clearly and distinctly perceive is of necessity true: although I no longer attend to the grounds of a judgment, no opposite reason can be alleged sufficient to lead me to doubt of its truth, provided only I remember that I once possessed a clear and distinct comprehension of it. My knowledge of it thus becomes true and certain. And this same knowledge extends likewise to whatever I remember to have formerly demonstrated, as the truths of geometry and the like: for what can be alleged against them to lead me to doubt of them? Will it be that my nature is such that I may be frequently deceived? But I already know that I cannot be deceived in judgments of the grounds of which I possess a clear knowledge. Will it be that I formerly deemed things to be true and certain which I afterward discovered to be false? But I had no clear and distinct knowledge of any of those things, and, being as yet ignorant of the rule by which I am assured of the truth of a judgment, I was led to give my assent to them on grounds which I afterward discovered were less strong than at the time I imagined them to be. What further objection, then, is there? Will it be said that perhaps I am dreaming (an objection I lately myself raised), or that all the thoughts of which I am now conscious have no more truth than the reveries of my dreams? But although, in truth, I should be dreaming, the rule still holds that all which is clearly presented to my intellect is indisputably true.

sure about something and it ended up being completely wrong after all. How embarrassing, right?

— **15**

But now I know God exists and He isn't a deceiver and everything is cool with Him, and also that clear and distinct perceptions are true. I don't have to bother remembering the exact proof for something, as long as I remember that there *is* a proof or even just that once I understood this thing clearly and distinctly. Finally I'm getting somewhere: I found a way to know everything I ever need to know.

Right? I mean, what's supposed to be the problem with trusting clear and distinct perceptions? That I'm *super* easy to lie to? No shit, but now I know that there are certain things I can't be deceived about: things I perceive clearly and distinctly. Or what about how I *frequently* used to believe things that turned out to be false? "That's Paul Rabil over there." "Families always live together." "It's what you know that matters." All that shit, I believed without clear and distinct knowledge; I formed those beliefs on muddled and half-ass evidence. I was wrong to believe them, but now I know better. I know to stick to clear and distinct perceptions. What about how I could be in a dream or a 'shroom trip or some kind of drunken stupor where I perceive crazy false shit and I want to just believe all of it? That could be true but it wouldn't affect the fact that I can believe my clear and distinct perceptions. As long as I stick to clear and distinct perceptions, I won't believe any bullshit dream logic where my teeth are falling out but my smile is still great, or I'm naked in front of an audience and it's a *bad* thing for some reason, but I'll still be able to believe in like triangles and shit. Even in dreams, triangles have 180 degrees, motherfuckers.

16 —

And thus I very clearly see that the certitude and truth of all science depends on the knowledge alone of the true God, insomuch that, before I knew him, I could have no perfect knowledge of any other thing. And now that I know him, I possess the means of acquiring a perfect knowledge respecting innumerable matters, as well relative to God himself and other intellectual objects as to corporeal nature, in so far as it is the object of pure mathematics [which do not consider whether it exists or not].

WHAT DID OUR HERO ACCOMPLISH TODAY, AND HOW DOES IT FIT INTO HIS PROJECT THIS WEEK?

— **16**

Hot damn, this has been a productive day. Earlier, when I hadn't figured out that God exists, I didn't know shit. Now that I'm sure God is real, I can trust my clear and distinct perceptions, and *that* lets me know tons of other shit. Things like God, mathematics, even physical bodies with mathematical shapes. I can be sure that the *shape* of my rectangular towel has four right angles, even if the towel itself is just an illusion. Knowing that God exists makes it so much easier to know other shit! Man, I'm feeling good.

Now that I understand how to derive knowledge from other knowledge, I'm pretty much home free. So here's the plan for tonight: I'mma get fucked up and not worry too much about the consequences, because I know how to figure them out as I go. I am fucking stoked to be done with the shitty parts of this week. I want to get to the part where I figure a bunch of shit out and have a good-ass time. After all, YOLO. Probably. Right? Fuck.

MEDITATION VI

. . .

Of The Existence of Material Things, And of The Real Distinction Between The Mind And Body of Man.

01

There now only remains the inquiry as to whether material things exist. With regard to this question, I at least know with certainty that such things may exist, in as far as they constitute the object of the pure mathematics, since, regarding them in this aspect, I can conceive them clearly and distinctly. For there can be no doubt that God possesses the power of producing all the objects I am able distinctly to conceive, and I never considered anything impossible to him, unless when I experienced a contradiction in the attempt to conceive it aright. Further, the faculty of imagination which I possess, and of which I am conscious that I make use when I apply myself to the consideration of material things, is sufficient to persuade me of their existence: for, when I attentively consider what imagination is, I find that it is simply a certain application of the cognitive faculty (*facultas cognoscitiva*) to a body which is immediately present to it, and which therefore exists.

WHAT IS OUR HERO'S GOAL IN THIS LAST MEDITATION?

MEDITATION VI

. . .

Of The Existence of Material Things, And of The Real Distinction Between The Mind And Body of Man.

— **01**

Uuuugh I can't believe I'm hungover again; I was hoping I could use my knowledge of material objects to avoid this situation. I guess I only got as far as proving the existence of, like, *mathematical triangles* and shit, and that's not enough; I need to figure out whether anything physical *actually* exists. I have *so goddamn many* ideas about material shit, and it sure would be swell to know if any of it is really out there. I can't stop this hangover, but if I can figure out if my body is real or not *now*, maybe I can prevent future hangover-type disasters. Obviously it's *possible* that material things exist, since nothing I can think of is impossible for God unless there's some sort of *logical contradiction* I run into when I try to think of it. Maybe things like "has corners and no corners" or "Hey, I don't mean to brag." are a problem for God, but a velvet-covered triangular table isn't. There's no contradiction in that idea, even though it's new-money as shit.

I also wonder about the power of imagination. I have this mental power to think about a body that I'm picturing *right there in front of my mind*, but a body can't be in front of the mind if it doesn't exist, right? If I'm picturing butts—butts of *all kinds*—then in some sense those butts exist, *right??*

02

And to render this quite clear, I remark, in the first place, the difference that subsists between imagination and pure intellection [or conception]. For example, when I imagine a triangle I not only conceive (*intelligo*) that it is a figure comprehended by three lines, but at the same time also I look upon (*intueor*) these three lines as present by the power and internal application of my mind (*acie mentis*), and this is what I call imagining. But if I desire to think of a chiliogon, I indeed rightly conceive that it is a figure composed of a thousand sides, as easily as I conceive that a triangle is a figure composed of only three sides; but I cannot imagine the thousand sides of a chiliogon as I do the three sides of a triangle, nor, so to speak, view them as present [with the eyes of my mind]. And although, in accordance with the habit I have of always imagining something when I think of corporeal things, it may happen that, in conceiving a chiliogon, I confusedly represent some figure to myself, yet it is quite evident that this is not a chiliogon, since it in no wise differs from that which I would represent to myself, if I were to think of a myriogon, or any other figure of many sides; nor would this representation be of any use in discovering and unfolding the properties that constitute the difference between a chiliogon and other polygons. But if the question turns on a pentagon, it is quite true that I can conceive its figure, as well as that of a chiliogon, without the aid of imagination; but I can likewise imagine it by applying the attention of my mind to its five sides, and at the same time to the area which they contain. Thus I observe that a special effort of mind is necessary to the act of imagination, which is not required to conceiving or understanding (*ad intelligendum*); and this special exertion of mind clearly shows the difference between imagination and pure intellection (*imaginatio et intellectio pura*).

— 02

Imagining butts isn't the same as *conceiving* butts; conceiving is like the Bud Light of thinking: it's your basic, simple, everyday-get-it-done mental power. Conceiving is really as simple as *thinking about something* or *holding an idea in my mind. Imagining* is more like Bud Light Platinum: it's an even more expensive version of the thing I love. It includes conceiving, but there's more to it than that. When I imagine something, I form a mental picture in front of my "mind's eye." I can conceive of a triangle by just thinking about a triangle, saying to myself, "Triangles. Sure, I've heard of those," but I'm not really *picturing* a triangle. When I imagine a triangle, I *am* picturing a triangle in my mind.

So let's say I think about a thousand-sided shape; that's easy enough to *conceive*, but I can't exactly picture *all one thousand fucking sides.* I end up picturing something with too many sides to count but it's probably only like 50, or else I just get like a grainy-ass circle. Then if I try to picture a shape with 1001 sides, maybe I can picture one side getting added on, but I get basically the same thing: it looks like a circle on a shitty monitor with bad graphics. If I wanted to prove the interior angles in a shape with 1000 sides are different from the interior angles in a shape with 1001 sides, those mental pictures would be fucking useless. It's like, "Fuck it, this is exhausting and not worth it. I'll just use the equations." Even picturing a simple triangle takes some concentration, so forget about doing it with crazy complicated shapes. That's one really easy way to understand the difference between imagination and conception: imagination requires effort in a way that conception doesn't.

03

I remark, besides, that this power of imagination which I possess, in as far as it differs from the power of conceiving, is in no way necessary to my [nature or] essence, that is, to the essence of my mind; for although I did not possess it, I should still remain the same that I now am, from which it seems we may conclude that it depends on something different from the mind. And I easily understand that, if some body exists, with which my mind is so conjoined and united as to be able, as it were, to consider it when it chooses, it may thus imagine corporeal objects; so that this mode of thinking differs from pure intellection only in this respect, that the mind in conceiving turns in some way upon itself, and considers some one of the ideas it possesses within itself; but in imagining it turns toward the body, and contemplates in it some object conformed to the idea which it either of itself conceived or apprehended by sense. I easily understand, I say, that imagination may be thus formed, if it is true that there are bodies; and because I find no other obvious mode of explaining it, I thence, with probability, conjecture that they exist, but only with probability; and although I carefully examine all things, nevertheless I do not find that, from the distinct idea of corporeal nature I have in my imagination, I can necessarily infer the existence of any body.

**WHY DOES OUR HERO THINK IMAGINATION AND BODIES MIGHT
BE CONNECTED?**

04

But I am accustomed to imagine many other objects besides that corporeal nature which is the object of the pure mathematics, as, for example, colors, sounds, tastes, pain, and the like, although with less distinctness; and, inasmuch as I perceive these objects much better by

— **03**

Here's another important difference between imagination and conception: conception is like a core part of my existence, but imagination isn't. Since conception is literally just thinking about a thing, I couldn't exist as a *thinking bro* without it. Without imagination, though, I would be basically the same dude, maybe with a slightly sadder childhood. I would still be able to think and doubt and prove things like normal, I just wouldn't be able to picture shit in my mind's eye. Since I don't need imagination to exist as a thinking bro, it isn't an essential part of my mind. Since imagination isn't an essential part of my mind, it must come from somewhere other than my mind.

Here's an idea, and I'm totally just throwing this out there: let's say there's some very handsome and muscular material body that my mind is joined to in some way. Let's just say. Maybe there's something about this totally-hypothetical, well-endowed body that the mind can use to form an actual sort of image. Like maybe the mind can take an idea and use the body somehow to turn that idea into an actual picture to look at.

I mean, there's definitely something *almost-physical* about the things I imagine, where the things seem to have real shape, and that would be easy to explain if my imagination came from a body. What's tricky here is that I don't know I have a body, but I also know that my imagination doesn't come from my mind, and it has to come from somewhere. Right now a body is the best explanation I can come up with, but I'm definitely not certain enough that I can just assume I have a body. For one thing, I'm not sure how almost-physical thoughts mean something actually physical has to exist.

— **04**

Of course, while I spend an awful lot of my Thursday nights imagining butts of various shapes, butts aren't *all* I have the power to imagine. I can also imagine weird colors and low, rumbling sounds, and sharp pain that hurts real good, and so on, all of which keep those Thursday nights from

the senses, through the medium of which and of memory, they seem
to have reached the imagination, I believe that, in order the more ad-
vantageously to examine them, it is proper I should at the same time
examine what sense-perception is, and inquire whether from those
ideas that are apprehended by this mode of thinking (consciousness),
I cannot obtain a certain proof of the existence of corporeal objects.

05 —

And, in the first place, I will recall to my mind the things I have hitherto held as true, because perceived by the senses, and the foundations
upon which my belief in their truth rested; I will, in the second place,
examine the reasons that afterward constrained me to doubt of them;
and, finally, I will consider what of them I ought now to believe.

06 —

Firstly, then, I perceived that I had a head, hands, feet and other members composing that body which I considered as part, or perhaps even
as the whole, of myself. I perceived further, that that body was placed
among many others, by which it was capable of being affected in diverse ways, both beneficial and hurtful; and what was beneficial I remarked by a certain sensation of pleasure, and what was hurtful by a
sensation of pain. And besides this pleasure and pain, I was likewise
conscious of hunger, thirst, and other appetites, as well as certain corporeal inclinations toward joy, sadness, anger, and similar passions.
And, out of myself, besides the extension, figure, and motions of bodies, I likewise perceived in them hardness, heat, and the other tactile
qualities, and, in addition, light, colors, odors, tastes, and sounds, the
variety of which gave me the means of distinguishing the sky, the
earth, the sea, and generally all the other bodies, from one another.
And certainly, considering the ideas of all these qualities, which were
presented to my mind, and which alone I properly and immediately

falling into a boring routine. It's important to keep it fresh for yourself. Obviously those things come through much more clearly when I use my senses than my imagination, and (as is SO OFTEN true of my Thursday night ritual) they probably even *started* as things I learned with my senses and then "passed on" to the imagination, which means in order to fully understand my imagination I *also* have to spend some time thinking about my senses.

— **05**

Fuck, just when I thought I was almost done with this stupid fucking problem, it turns out I have to go back over everything I ever learned about with my senses and figure out why I decided to *stop* believing those things, so that I can decide which of those things I can go *back* to believing in.

— **06**

Ugh, holy *shit* is there a lot of stuff I supposedly learned about through the senses.

There's the fact that I have a body composed of a head, hands, feet and other "members." There's the fact that in some way I *am* a body at all. There's the fact that there are other bodies all over the place that can interact with my body. Sometimes those interactions are good, in which case I feel pleasure and it's awesome and I'm drunk, and sometimes those interactions are bad and hurt a lot and no insurance settlement can ever bring Chad back. There's pleasure and pain, hunger and thirst, there's joy and sadness and anger, and I don't just *think* those things: I feel them, physically, *in my body* somehow. I've had moments of being so happy it felt like my heart could bust a nut, and moments so terrifying I thought the only thing keeping my stomach inside my body was my valiant asshole. There's everything the senses told me about these bodies: these bodies supposedly have extension in space and shape and movement, but they also have qualities you can feel like

perceived, it was not without reason that I thought I perceived certain objects wholly different from my thought, namely, bodies from which those ideas proceeded; for I was conscious that the ideas were presented to me without my consent being required, so that I could not perceive any object, however desirous I might be, unless it were present to the organ of sense; and it was wholly out of my power not to perceive it when it was thus present. And because the ideas I perceived by the senses were much more lively and clear, and even, in their own way, more distinct than any of those I could of myself frame by meditation, or which I found impressed on my memory, it seemed that they could not have proceeded from myself, and must therefore have been caused in me by some other objects; and as of those objects I had no knowledge beyond what the ideas themselves gave me, nothing was so likely to occur to my mind as the supposition that the objects were similar to the ideas which they caused. And because I recollected also that I had formerly trusted to the senses, rather than to reason, and that the ideas which I myself formed were not so clear as those I perceived by sense, and that they were even for the most part composed of parts of the latter, I was readily persuaded that I had no idea in my intellect which had not formerly passed through the senses. Nor was I altogether wrong in likewise believing that that body which, by a special right, I called my own, pertained to me more properly and strictly than any of the others; for in truth, I could never be separated from it as from other bodies; I felt in it and on account of it all my appetites and affections, and in fine I was affected in its parts by pain and the titillation of pleasure, and not in the parts of the other bodies that were separated from it. But when I inquired into the reason why, from this I know not what sensation of pain, sadness of mind should follow, and why from the sensation of pleasure, joy should arise, or why this indescribable twitching of the stomach, which I call hunger, should put me in mind of taking food, and the parchedness of the throat of drink, and so in other cases, I was unable to give any explanation, un-

hardness and heat, and qualities you can sense like color and odor and taste and sound. Different bodies have different qualities, so the fact that some things are dark and some things are light let me tell the difference between the ocean and the sand, between rum and vodka, between whiskey and cheap whiskey.

I mean, I know how fucking naïve that sounds now, but when I think about how vibrant all those qualities seem, I... I can hardly blame myself for thinking it was the objects themselves I perceived, rather than just the ideas of those objects. It's not like I wanted to perceive everything so badly that I just made it all up; my will was completely out of the picture here. Some shit was presented to my senses, and I perceived it whether or not I wanted to. Even when I was like "Boy, sure would be nice to perceive a frosty cold brew" nothing changed for my senses no matter how badly I wanted it. I tried wishing, imagining, picturing, meditating on, and *remembering* a cold brew; I tried everything that my will *could* be involved in, and still I didn't perceive it *nearly* as clearly as I perceived the things that were actually presented to my senses. So yeah, excuse me, I was convinced that my sensory ideas couldn't have come from me.

Of course, I also used to think that my senses were the key to knowledge. Now I know that using *reason* is the most fundamental part of knowing anything, but back then I thought that my mental ideas were cobbled together from pictures I saw with my eyes. Like I'd *see* a butt and that's how I got my entire idea of butts; in fact, I used to think that deep down, *all* of my ideas came through my senses one way or another.

Which, yeah, that's an *insane* amount of faith to put in my senses, but if I look at it from the perspective of past-me, it makes sense. I have this body that always seems to be around, and I've poured tons of effort into making it as rock-hard and godly-bronzed as possible, and it seemed to be working. No wonder I assumed my senses were reliable, right? I mean, no matter what else I perceive, this stupid studly meatbag is always *right the fuck there*, and whenever I feel pleasure or pain it's always through *this specific meatbag*. But that doesn't explain why pleasure makes

less that I was so taught by nature; for there is assuredly no affinity, at least none that I am able to comprehend, between this irritation of the stomach and the desire of food, any more than between the perception of an object that causes pain and the consciousness of sadness which springs from the perception. And in the same way it seemed to me that all the other judgments I had formed regarding the objects of sense, were dictates of nature; because I remarked that those judgments were formed in me, before I had leisure to weigh and consider the reasons that might constrain me to form them.

07 —

But, afterward, a wide experience by degrees sapped the faith I had reposed in my senses; for I frequently observed that towers, which at a distance seemed round, appeared square, when more closely viewed, and that colossal figures, raised on the summits of these towers, looked like small statues, when viewed from the bottom of them; and, in other instances without number, I also discovered error in judgments founded on the external senses; and not only in those founded on the external, but even in those that rested on the internal senses; for is there aught more internal than pain? And yet I have sometimes been informed by parties whose arm or leg had been amputated, that they still occasionally seemed to feel pain in that part of the body which they had lost,—a circumstance that led me to think that I could not be quite certain even that any one of my members was affected when I felt pain in it. And to these grounds of doubt I shortly afterward also added two others of very wide generality: the first of them was that I believed I never perceived anything when awake which I could not occasionally think I also perceived when asleep, and as I do

me happy, why hunger makes me want to eat, why sadness makes me want to drink, and so on, unless that is just somehow part of my nature. It just *happens to be true* about me, without any further explanation. Just, "That's the way it is, kiddo!" because I don't see any other reason why the two should be connected; what do pain and sadness, pleasure and joy have in common? Or the feeling of hunger and a desire to eat? It's like, "Okay, my body feels a way. So what? Now all of a sudden my mind is making a judgment?" Just because my body is all "Ow that hurts," I just *decide* in my mind that "Oh, I should avoid getting punched in the dick?" That connection has to be somehow built into me or given to me by nature or something like that; it's just somehow *an instinct I have*, because I sure as shit never came up with arguments or reasons to trust my senses like that.

— **07**

...which is how I ended up on the most wretched, terrifying fucking Spring Break of my life. You can only mistake a guy with a real crispy flow and a tank top for Paul Rabil and then drunkenly blow your Spring Break budget on bottle service so many times before it's like, "Ah, shit, maybe my senses are unreliable after all?" Fuck, and maybe it's not just external senses that are unreliable; I remember that soldier I was buying drinks for in the airport telling me about how he sometimes feels pain in his leg, except, holy shit, he was missing the leg. That's fucking insane, right? "I'm hurting in a part of my body that literally doesn't exist." What the fuck. So now when my leg feels pain, I'm like, "Shit, am I sure I *have* a leg?"

And then there's that thing where I see crazy ideas in my dreams, and those ideas don't come from anything external. Why should I assume my waking experience is any different? When I'm asleep and I perceive all my teeth turning into mice, there's no external *tooth-mice*. Teeth-mouse. Teeth-mice? Whatever. There's no external object that perception matches up with. Why should my perceptions correspond to anything while I'm awake?

not believe that the ideas I seem to perceive in my sleep proceed from objects external to me, I did not any more observe any ground for believing this of such as I seem to perceive when awake; the second was that since I was as yet ignorant of the author of my being or at least supposed myself to be so, I saw nothing to prevent my having been so constituted by nature as that I should be deceived even in matters that appeared to me to possess the greatest truth. And, with respect to the grounds on which I had before been persuaded of the existence of sensible objects, I had no great difficulty in finding suitable answers to them; for as nature seemed to incline me to many things from which reason made me averse, I thought that I ought not to confide much in its teachings. And although the perceptions of the senses were not dependent on my will, I did not think that I ought on that ground to conclude that they proceeded from things different from myself, since perhaps there might be found in me some faculty, though hitherto unknown to me, which produced them.

08 —

But now that I begin to know myself better, and to discover more clearly the author of my being, I do not, indeed, think that I ought rashly to admit all which the senses seem to teach, nor, on the other hand, is it my conviction that I ought to doubt in general of their teachings.

09 —

And, firstly, because I know that all which I clearly and distinctly conceive can be produced by God exactly as I conceive it, it is sufficient that I am able clearly and distinctly to conceive one thing apart from another, in order to be certain that the one is different from the other, seeing they may at least be made to exist separately, by the omnipotence of God; and it matters not by what power this separation is made, in order to be compelled to judge them different; and, there-

Oh, and while I'm piling shit on, let's not forget that until I knew God existed, I had no reason to believe in what seemed clear and distinct to me; like, as far as I knew, maybe I was wrong about even the *most obvious things*.

So, I mean, maybe my "first instinct" is to believe my senses, but my first instinct is also to literally just shit my pants whenever I'm drunk. I have no idea, really, whether my sensory ideas come from things *outside* of myself; sure, I didn't *choose* to perceive these sensory ideas, but as far as I know they come from another power within me I don't even realize I have.

WHAT TWO WAYS OF "TRUSTING HIS SENSES" DOES OUR HERO TALK ABOUT IN 06 AND 07?

08

But now that I've spent five real careful, boring, shitty days figuring out how knowledge works and that God exists and all that, I'm not sure my senses are *totally* worthless. It would be stupid to dive right-the-fuck back in and take *every sensory idea* seriously, but maybe some of my sensory ideas have *some* value.

09

After all, God *could* produce anything that I have a clear and distinct perception of. So if I can clearly, distinctly perceive one thing without the other thing being there, God could make that happen. For example, I clearly, distinctly understand myself as a thinking thing, and my body doesn't have shit to do with it, which means that my mind doesn't need my body to exist; God could create me without a body if He wanted to. He could also make my body without my mind—I don't know *why* He

fore, merely because I know with certitude that I exist, and because, in the meantime, I do not observe that aught necessarily belongs to my nature or essence beyond my being a thinking thing, I rightly conclude that my essence consists only in my being a thinking thing [or a substance whose whole essence or nature is merely thinking]. And although I may, or rather, as I will shortly say, although I certainly do possess a body with which I am very closely conjoined; nevertheless, because, on the one hand, I have a clear and distinct idea of myself, in as far as I am only a thinking and unextended thing, and as, on the other hand, I possess a distinct idea of body, in as far as it is only an extended and unthinking thing, it is certain that I, [that is, my mind, by which I am what I am], is entirely and truly distinct from my body, and may exist without it.

10 —

Moreover, I find in myself diverse faculties of thinking that have each their special mode: for example, I find I possess the faculties of imagining and perceiving, without which I can indeed clearly and distinctly conceive myself as entire, but I cannot reciprocally conceive them without conceiving myself, that is to say, without an intelligent substance in which they reside, for [in the notion we have of them, or to use the terms of the schools] in their formal concept, they comprise some sort of intellection; whence I perceive that they are distinct from myself as modes are from things. I remark likewise certain other faculties, as the power of changing place, of assuming diverse figures, and the like, that cannot be conceived and cannot therefore exist, any more than the preceding, apart from a substance in which they inhere. It is very evident, however, that these faculties, if they really exist, must belong to some corporeal or extended substance, since in their clear and distinct concept there is contained some sort of extension, but no intellection at all. Further, I cannot doubt but that there is in me a certain passive faculty of perception, that is, of receiving and

would waste this incredible body like that, it feels like someone should get to enjoy such a work of art, but He *could*. Since my body and my mind could exist without each other, *they're obviously not the same thing*. Since I can conceive of myself existing without a body, my body isn't essential to *who I am*. I'm not just a piece of meat; in fact, I exist totally independently of *all pieces of meat*.

WHY IS IT IMPORTANT THAT SOME OF OUR HERO'S POWERS ARE NOT ESSENTIAL TO HIS IDENTITY?

— 10

I can also conceive of myself without some of the powers I have, like imagination and sensory perception. Like, if I lost those, I wouldn't stop existing or being a thinking thing, I just wouldn't have any imagination anymore. So that power isn't *essential* to me, and the *power* of imagination is different from me, the *thing* with imagination. There are other powers too, like the power to *be in the shape of a fist*. That power is different from the thing *in* the shape of a fist. Powers can't just float around out there on their own. A power needs to live in something. Could be a hand, could be a statue, could be a dildo; those all have the power to be shaped like a fist. But not everything has the power to be shaped like a fist. Different powers live in different kinds of things, and only material bodies have the power to be in the shape of a fist. Obviously I can't say, "My mind is in the shape of a fist." Maybe I'm angry or some shit but minds can't have shapes, since being *non-physical* is part of what it means to be a mind.

Anyway, that's the difference between powers and the things that have them.

taking knowledge of the ideas of sensible things; but this would be useless to me, if there did not also exist in me, or in some other thing, another active faculty capable of forming and producing those ideas. But this active faculty cannot be in me [in as far as I am but a thinking thing], seeing that it does not presuppose thought, and also that those ideas are frequently produced in my mind without my contributing to it in any way, and even frequently contrary to my will. This faculty must therefore exist in some substance different from me, in which all the objective reality of the ideas that are produced by this faculty is contained formally or eminently, as I before remarked; and this substance is either a body, that is to say, a corporeal nature in which is contained formally [and in effect] all that is objectively [and by representation] in those ideas; or it is God Himself, or some other creature, of a rank superior to body, in which the same is contained eminently. But as God is no deceiver, it is manifest that He does not of Himself and immediately communicate those ideas to me, nor even by the intervention of any creature in which their objective reality is not formally, but only eminently, contained. For as He has given me no faculty whereby I can discover this to be the case, but, on the contrary, a very strong inclination to believe that those ideas arise from corporeal objects, I do not see how He could be vindicated from the charge of deceit, if in truth they proceeded from any other source, or were produced by other causes than corporeal things: and accordingly it must be concluded, that corporeal objects exist. Nevertheless, they are not perhaps exactly such as we perceive by the senses, for their comprehension by the senses is, in many instances, very obscure and confused; but it is at least necessary to admit that all which I clearly and distinctly conceive as in them, that is, generally speaking all that is comprehended in the object of speculative geometry, really exists external to me.

So my mind has this power to receive sensory ideas. It's a passive power that just receives whatever sensory ideas get sent to it, but those ideas have to come from somewhere. There must be some source with the active power to *produce* those ideas. The source can't be me, because I'm just a thinking thing, and *producing* ideas doesn't require me to think at all. Even dirt or those shitty kids playing over there can be sources of color and noise. Plus if I had the power to produce ideas, it seems like I should have at least a little bit of control over what gets produced, and I totally don't.

So the power to produce ideas has to live in something else. What kind of thing does it live in? Well, the source is producing ideas that have objective reality, so it has to have quite a bit of formal reality. Maybe the source of my sensory ideas *resembles* those ideas in some way: some of the ideas I'm receiving contain the objective reality of butts, so if the ideas resemble the sources, the sources are butts themselves. Or maybe the Source doesn't have a butt, but it is powerful enough to *create* butts. So that would mean the Source is God or one of His angels or something, and He's producing *ideas* of butts directly without bothering to create the butts themselves.

Okay, I can feel this slipping away from me and into "blame-God territory" again, so lemme just make sure I'm with it so far: the ideas I perceive with my senses have to come from something. That something isn't me, because producing ideas doesn't require me to think, which is all I can do; it's gotta be either God or bodies, because only God or bodies could have the right kinds of reality to produce sensory ideas.

The thing is that I have this really strong inclination to believe that the idea of a butt does, in fact, come from a real butt. Like there's some physical, real butt broadcasting the idea of that butt. If God gave me this strong inclination, and it's *false*, He would have to give me some way to correct it, or else He would be a deceiver, right? But I have no way whatsoever to tell whether the butt actually exists or God is just planting the idea of a butt in my mind directly, since I can't interact *directly* with

10 IS A REALLY IMPORTANT PARAGRAPH YOU SHOULD OUTLINE HERE.

11 —

But with respect to other things which are either only particular, as, for example, that the sun is of such a size and figure, etc., or are conceived with less clearness and distinctness, as light, sound, pain, and the like, although they are highly dubious and uncertain, nevertheless on the ground alone that God is no deceiver, and that consequently he has permitted no falsity in my opinions which he has not likewise given me a faculty of correcting, I think I may with safety conclude that I possess in myself the means of arriving at the truth. And, in the first place, it cannot be doubted that in each of the dictates of nature there is some truth: for by nature, considered in general, I now understand nothing more than God Himself, or the order and disposition established by God in created things; and by my nature in particular I understand the assemblage of all that God has given me.

butts; my *several* butt-related interactions a week always and only take place through ideas. Since God definitely isn't a deceiver, my inclination to assume butt-ideas correspond to physical butts must be correct: that idea of a butt must actually come from a butt of some sort.

Oh, holy shit. And once I know "The power to broadcast sensory ideas lives in a body or bodies," then I also know "Oh, yeah, obviously those bodies also exist." So there must actually be material things! Maybe those bodies aren't exactly like the ideas I have of them; like maybe not every butt is exactly as firm as it feels, right? The senses are unreliable, and maybe butts are weird in ways I can't tell. But holy fuck, what a huge relief to know that those butts at least *exist*. And at least I can be sure that butts follow the rules I clearly and distinctly perceive, like geometry and shit; there aren't any square butts that are also circular butts. Even if those butts are weird, they're not so weird they violate math.

— **11**

Still, I have to be careful not to assume anything uncertain about bodies. What the fuck do I actually know about them? They sure do produce a shitload of ideas for me to perceive, but those ideas are all kinds of fuzzy. How big is the sun? What shape is it? What the fuck was that noise? Questions are many! Answers are few! But I know from day Four that God wouldn't let me make a mistake that I couldn't *somehow* correct—if I can fuck it up, I can also fix it. Besides, whatever nature teaches me has to have *some* truth to it—after all, "nature" is just God Himself and the order He created, and my "nature" is just everything God has given me. So every part of my nature has to teach me *something*. There can't be any parts of my nature that are *total* garbage.

12 —

But there is nothing which that nature teaches me more expressly [or more sensibly] than that I have a body which is ill affected when I feel pain, and stands in need of food and drink when I experience the sensations of hunger and thirst, etc. And therefore I ought not to doubt but that there is some truth in these informations.

13 —

Nature likewise teaches me by these sensations of pain, hunger, thirst, etc., that I am not only lodged in my body as a pilot in a vessel, but that I am besides so intimately conjoined, and as it were intermixed with it, that my mind and body compose a certain unity. For if this were not the case, I should not feel pain when my body is hurt, seeing I am merely a thinking thing, but should perceive the wound by the understanding alone, just as a pilot perceives by sight when any part of his vessel is damaged; and when my body has need of food or drink, I should have a clear knowledge of this, and not be made aware of it by the confused sensations of hunger and thirst: for, in truth, all these sensations of hunger, thirst, pain, etc., are nothing more than certain confused modes of thinking, arising from the union and apparent fusion of mind and body.

14 —

Besides this, nature teaches me that my own body is surrounded by many other bodies, some of which I have to seek after, and others to

— **12**

You know one thing my nature teaches me? I have this super-duper meat husk that is very impressive but also requires an awful lot of maintenance. Nature teaches me that whenever I feel pain that means my body got messed up a little, and whenever I get hungry I should interrupt important game-spitting and sports-doing to shovel food into my face, which happens three to seven times a day. There must be *some* truth to that connection between feeling pain and being injured, or feeling hunger and needing food, since it comes from my nature.

— **13**

Nature *also* teaches me that I don't just *have* this body; I'm *connected* to it in some way. I'm not just *driving* this thing around and I can get out whenever I want. It's not like if my body were on fire, I would just be like, "Ah shit, dad's Beamer is on fire again. I should try to fix that so he doesn't know I borrowed it." If I were on fire, I'd be more like "AAAAHHHH, AHH-HHH, AHHHHHHHH, AAAAAAAHHHHHH." When I need food and drink, I don't get a cute little light on a dashboard like "Hey, running low on fuel here!" Instead, when I'm hungry or thirsty my body just *kind of starts to feel weird*, and then it slows down a bunch and I can't focus, but I have to figure out for myself that "Oh, I should probably eat something."

It's like my mind and body are *blended together* somehow, and modes of thought like hunger or thirst or pain don't arise just in the body or just in the mind (the way that, say, thoughts about math arise just in the mind); they arise specifically from the *blend* of the two. It's like how Jager gets you drunk, and Red Bull makes you hype, but making me an absolute party-fuck-machine doesn't come from one or the other but the *combination*.

— **14**

My nature also teaches me that the bodies that appear differently to my senses must be different in other ways, too. Like, if I see two butts and

shun. And indeed, as I perceive different sorts of colors, sounds, odors, tastes, heat, hardness, etc., I safely conclude that there are in the bodies from which the diverse perceptions of the senses proceed, certain varieties corresponding to them, although, perhaps, not in reality like them; and since, among these diverse perceptions of the senses, some are agreeable, and others disagreeable, there can be no doubt that my body, or rather my entire self, in as far as I am composed of body and mind, may be variously affected, both beneficially and hurtfully, by surrounding bodies.

WHAT SHOULDN'T OUR HERO TRUST HIS SENSES TO TELL HIM?

15 —

But there are many other beliefs which though seemingly the teaching of nature, are not in reality so, but which obtained a place in my mind through a habit of judging inconsiderately of things. It may thus easily happen that such judgments shall contain error: thus, for example, the opinion I have that all space in which there is nothing to affect [or make an impression on] my senses is void: that in a hot body there is something in every respect similar to the idea of heat in my mind; that in a white or green body there is the same whiteness or greenness which I perceive; that in a bitter or sweet body there is the same taste, and so in other instances; that the stars, towers, and all distant bodies, are of the same size and figure as they appear to our eyes, etc. But that I may avoid everything like indistinctness of conception, I must accurately define what I properly understand by being taught by nature. For nature is here taken in a narrower sense than when it signifies the sum of all the things which God has given me; seeing that in that

I'm like "This butt looks good, that butt looks good but in a different way," there must be *some* difference in the butts themselves that makes them *appear* differently to my senses.

I also know that the different bodies around me can affect me in a variety of ways. For example, some of the bodies around me (like kegs) are good for me, while other bodies around me (like sharks) are bad for me; I know that because my senses react pleasantly to keg stands and really poorly to shark attacks. It's like what happened after that trip to Cabo, and now when I smell tequila I'm like "oh god, imma throw up, oh fuck," and my body just knows to make a beeline for a toilet bowl. My mind and body react that way to remind me that tequila will absolutely fucking ruin my day. These modes of thought that come from the blending of mind and body (like pleasure and pain, hunger and thirst, nausea and boners) tell me how other bodies will affect me in some way: some bodies are good for me, others are tequila-sharks.

— **15**

But even though my nature teaches me a bunch of shit about how other bodies affect me, a bunch of stuff about my *relationship* to different bodies, I have to be careful to not assume that my nature teaches me anything about those bodies themselves. Like, if my senses don't detect anything in a space, that doesn't mean that space isn't actually full of air or ghosts. Or if a body feels hot to me, I shouldn't assume there's such a thing as actual heat that perfectly corresponds to what I'm feeling in the body. Or if a body appears white or green to me, I don't know that the body really is white or green exactly the way it appears to me. Or if a food tastes bitter or sweet to me, I can't be sure there is some bitterness or sweetness in the actual food that corresponds exactly to the way I perceive it. It's like how I can cover the entire sun with my hand so I can't see it anymore and it doesn't get in my eyes, but I still don't know that the sun is exactly as small as it looks.

There's nothing in my nature that tells me how the external world

meaning the notion comprehends much that belongs only to the mind
[to which I am not here to be understood as referring when I use the
term nature]; as, for example, the notion I have of the truth, that what
is done cannot be undone, and all the other truths I discern by the
natural light [without the aid of the body]; and seeing that it comprehends likewise much besides that belongs only to body, and is not here
any more contained under the name nature, as the quality of heavi-
ness, and the like, of which I do not speak, the term being reserved
exclusively to designate the things which God has given to me as a
being composed of mind and body. But nature, taking the term in the
sense explained, teaches me to shun what causes in me the sensation
of pain, and to pursue what affords me the sensation of pleasure, and
other things of this sort; but I do not discover that it teaches me, in
addition to this, from these diverse perceptions of the senses, to draw
any conclusions respecting external objects without a previous [care-
ful and mature] consideration of them by the mind: for it is, as appears
to me, the office of the mind alone, and not of the composite whole of
mind and body, to discern the truth in those matters. Thus, although
the impression a star makes on my eye is not larger than that from the
flame of a candle, I do not, nevertheless, experience any real or positive impulse determining me to believe that the star is not greater
than the flame; the true account of the matter being merely that I have
so judged from my youth without any rational ground. And, though on
approaching the fire I feel heat, and even pain on approaching it too
closely, I have, however, from this no ground for holding that something resembling the heat I feel is in the fire, any more than that there
is something similar to the pain; all that I have ground for believing is,
that there is something in it, whatever it may be, which excites in me
those sensations of heat or pain. So also, although there are spaces in
which I find nothing to excite and affect my senses, I must not therefore conclude that those spaces contain in them no body; for I see that
in this, as in many other similar matters, I have been accustomed to

actually is; my nature only tells me how I should and shouldn't interact with the external world.

Or, at least, when I say "nature" here I mean my mind-body fusion. My *whole* nature includes the stuff that my mind teaches me without help from the body, like the existence of God or that contradictions can't be true, but I'm not talking about that right now. Right now I'm just trying to figure out what I can learn specifically from the cooperation of my body and mind.

When I focus in on only what my mind-body fusion teaches me, it's like, "Holy shit, this combination tells me almost nothing." Sure, I learn to avoid things that cause me pain and to chase things that cause me pleasure, but this mind-body fusion situation I've got going on teaches me precisely nothing about the *essential nature* of those things, and I was naïve to ever think I could learn anything essential through the senses. "Fire feels hot, so it must have heat in it." Oh really, past-me? Well, it also feels painful; does that mean that fire has pain in it? "That star and the light in that lighthouse look like they're the same size, so they must be." Holy fuck, *get a little closer to the lighthouse at all, asshole*, and look how much bigger it gets compared to the star. See how far off your senses were?

Obviously, I was misusing my senses before this week. Since they're part of my nature, they must have *some* truth to them: they're supposed to tell me what is harmful or helpful to this fusion thing I'm stuck in, and for *that* purpose, they are plenty clear and distinct. But what the fuck can my senses tell me about the essential nature of fire? Nothing. When I start using my senses to make judgments about the *actual nature* of things, I'm misusing something God gave me, and as I know already, that's how dudes end up trading dick pics with someone who isn't even Paul Rabil.

pervert the order of nature, because these perceptions of the senses, although given me by nature merely to signify to my mind what things are beneficial and hurtful to the composite whole of which it is a part, and being sufficiently clear and distinct for that purpose, are nevertheless used by me as infallible rules by which to determine immediately the essence of the bodies that exist out of me, of which they can of course afford me only the most obscure and confused knowledge.

16 —

But I have already sufficiently considered how it happens that, notwithstanding the supreme goodness of God, there is falsity in my judgments. A difficulty, however, here presents itself, respecting the things which I am taught by nature must be pursued or avoided, and also respecting the internal sensations in which I seem to have occasionally detected error, [and thus to be directly deceived by nature]: thus, for example, I may be so deceived by the agreeable taste of some viand with which poison has been mixed, as to be induced to take the poison. In this case, however, nature may be excused, for it simply leads me to desire the viand for its agreeable taste, and not the poison, which is unknown to it; and thus we can infer nothing from this circumstance beyond that our nature is not omniscient; at which there is assuredly no ground for surprise, since, man being of a finite nature, his knowledge must likewise be of a limited perfection.

17 —

But we also not unfrequently err in that to which we are directly impelled by nature, as is the case with invalids who desire drink or food that would be hurtful to them. It will here, perhaps, be alleged that the reason why such persons are deceived is that their nature is corrupted; but this leaves the difficulty untouched, for a sick man is not less really the creature of God than a man who is in full health; and therefore it is as repugnant to the goodness of God that the nature

WHAT SPECIFIC ROLE DO THE SENSES HAVE FOR OUR HERO?

— **16**

Wrong judgments are old news, and they definitely don't make God a deceiver. But if my senses are for deciding what is and isn't harmful and helpful, then what if someone smuggles poison into my post-hangover Gatorade, and I can't taste anything except those sweet, sweet electrolytes? I will fucking *crush* a Gatorade when I'm hungover, but now I'm chugging poison. Where the fuck are my senses now?

No, that's not a very good objection. It wasn't the poison my senses told me to drink; my nature tells me to drink beneficial things, like Gatorade, and that's what I did. The fact that the Gatorade was poisoned sucks, but it's not like my senses were like "Oh shit there's poison but keep going big guy, gotta rehydrate." My senses didn't even notice. All this tells me is that the senses aren't all-knowing, which, I mean, fucking surprise! My nature is limited; obviously, the shit I know is also limited.

— **17**

Okay, here's another objection, maybe: limited nature isn't always the problem; sometimes, my nature actively recommends something harmful. Like in high school, I used to beat up that kid with dropsy or *edema* or whatever it's called, that disease where parts of his body got swollen because his body wasn't processing water properly, so a shitload of water was just getting stored in his ankle. That kid got thirsty just like everyone else, which was his nature's way of getting him to drink water,

of the former should be deceitful as it is for that of the latter to be so. And as a clock, composed of wheels and counter weights, observes not the less accurately all the laws of nature when it is ill made, and points out the hours incorrectly, than when it satisfies the desire of the maker in every respect; so likewise if the body of man be considered as a kind of machine, so made up and composed of bones, nerves, muscles, veins, blood, and skin, that although there were in it no mind, it would still exhibit the same motions which it at present manifests involuntarily, and therefore without the aid of the mind, [and simply by the dispositions of its organs], I easily discern that it would also be as natural for such a body, supposing it dropsical, for example, to experience the parchedness of the throat that is usually accompanied in the mind by the sensation of thirst, and to be disposed by this parchedness to move its nerves and its other parts in the way required for drinking, and thus increase its malady and do itself harm, as it is natural for it, when it is not indisposed to be stimulated to drink for its good by a similar cause; and although looking to the use for which a clock was destined by its maker, I may say that it is deflected from its proper nature when it incorrectly indicates the hours, and on the same principle, considering the machine of the human body as having been formed by God for the sake of the motions which it usually manifests, although I may likewise have ground for thinking that it does not follow the order of its nature when the throat is parched and drink does not tend to its preservation, nevertheless I yet plainly discern that this latter acceptation of the term nature is very different from the other: for this is nothing more than a certain denomination, depending entirely on my thought, and hence called extrinsic, by which I compare a sick man and an imperfectly constructed clock with the idea I have of a man in good health and a well made clock; while by the other acceptation of nature is understood something which is truly found in things, and therefore possessed of some truth.

but *this fucking guy couldn't process water.* Seems like the failure of his nature was an *active* failure, where his nature specifically recommended something that actively harmed him.

And I can't just say, "Well, that dude just had a fucked-up nature, is all," because that raises a new question: how the fuck did his nature get corrupted? Shitty kids with dropsy are children of God, too, so why would He allow their nature to be corrupted?

So maybe his nature isn't corrupted after all; in fact, maybe he's actually following his nature. Maybe he's like a shitty knockoff Rolex you buy from some guy in an alley a couple blocks from whatever four-star hotel you're vacationing in, and for some reason it only takes 59 minutes for the minute hand to go all the way around, instead of a full hour. This watch still obeys its nature: the gears are poorly arranged, so the minute hand runs a little faster than expected and you have to keep resetting it, but the watch functions according to the laws of physics. It's a shitty watch, but it's not so shitty the *entire universe* is like "I have no idea what the fuck is going on here, that watch is magic but in a bad way." If you took the watch to a watchmaker, he'd be able to look at it and say, "Oh, the problem is just that some asshole made this watch so it completes a full circuit in 59 minutes. That's the nature of this watch." Ignoring the mind for a second and just looking at the body as a machine, it makes sense that the body obeys the laws of nature. When the body feels dry, there's an itching in the throat, and that triggers the "drink water" response. That's just how the body works, even if that person has dropsy.

I could ask this watchmaker, "Wait, is the watch *supposed* to go around all the way in 59 minutes? Isn't a watch supposed to measure a full hour?" But he might be like, "That depends on what you think a watch is for." If I say the "nature" of a watch is to measure an hour, then yeah, this watch deviates from its "nature," but maybe I'm wrong about what a watch is supposed to do. The watch doesn't deviate from how it was built, it only deviates from the purpose I want to assign it. Maybe for some people a watch that runs a minute fast every hour would be super

WHY IS IT IMPORTANT TO OUR HERO TO EXPLAIN WHY HIS SENSES
DON'T PROTECT HIM BETTER?

18 —

But certainly, although in respect of a dropsical body, it is only by way of exterior denomination that we say its nature is corrupted, when, without requiring drink, the throat is parched; yet, in respect of the composite whole, that is, of the mind in its union with the body, it is not a pure denomination, but really an error of nature, for it to feel thirst when drink would be hurtful to it: and, accordingly, it still remains to be considered why it is that the goodness of God does not prevent the nature of man thus taken from being fallacious.

19 —

To commence this examination accordingly, I here remark, in the first place, that there is a vast difference between mind and body, in respect that body, from its nature, is always divisible, and that mind is entirely indivisible. For in truth, when I consider the mind, that is, when I consider myself in so far only as I am a thinking thing, I can

useful, like if someone is constantly late all the time and it keeps them on schedule, or if you're trying to fuck with a pledge. A body with dropsy that drinks water anyway is just obeying physics, just like a watch with a minute hand that completes a circuit in the "wrong" time.

So while it's tempting to say that the "nature" of a watch is to show the right time and the "nature" of a body is to do what is healthiest, that's a different use of the word "nature" than I'm talking about here. That version of "nature" depends on some assumptions about the *purpose* of a watch or the human body, and right now I mean a nature that is *inherent to the thing*; a watch runs with whatever gears it has. That's the nature of a watch. A body's throat itches, and the body drinks; that's the nature of a body, even if it has dropsy.

— **18**

That explains why someone who has dropsy feels *thirsty* without his "nature" being *corrupted*, but when I add the mind back into the picture and consider the mind-body fusion, the problem returns: I get why the throat itches, but not why that throat itch makes the mind want water. The body isn't like a watch, which runs on its own; the body has someone driving it, and the driver's nature shouldn't be able to say "I know that fuel gauge is broken, but I really have the urge to put fuel in anyway." This is the sort of "nature" I've been dealing with this whole time: it's not a mechanical reaction, it's an intrinsic urge we all have to drink water when the throat itches. If that urge is toward something harmful, it's a problem, because it seems like it might make God a deceiver.

— **19**

Okay. Alright. I am right on the edge of something here, but I'm not sure what. If it turns out God is a deceiver after all, I am in a shitload of trouble. Let me back up and be real careful here.

So mind and body are different. Obviously, right? I've been over this a million fucking times. One important way they're different, though,

distinguish in myself no parts, but I very clearly discern that I am somewhat absolutely one and entire; and although the whole mind seems to be united to the whole body, yet, when a foot, an arm, or any other part is cut off, I am conscious that nothing has been taken from my mind; nor can the faculties of willing, perceiving, conceiving, etc., properly be called its parts, for it is the same mind that is exercised [all entire] in willing, in perceiving, and in conceiving, etc. But quite the opposite holds in corporeal or extended things; for I cannot imagine any one of them [how small soever it may be], which I cannot easily sunder in thought, and which, therefore, I do not know to be divisible. This would be sufficient to teach me that the mind or soul of man is entirely different from the body, if I had not already been apprised of it on other grounds.

20 —

I remark, in the next place, that the mind does not immediately receive the impression from all the parts of the body, but only from the brain, or perhaps even from one small part of it, viz, that in which the common sense (*senses communis*) is said to be, which as often as it is affected in the same way gives rise to the same perception in the mind, although meanwhile the other parts of the body may be diversely disposed, as is proved by innumerable experiments, which it is unnecessary here to enumerate.

WHAT IS OUR HERO TRYING TO EXPLAIN IN 19–23?

21 —

I remark, besides, that the nature of body is such that none of its parts can be moved by another part a little removed from the other, which

is that my mind is indivisible and my body is divisible. If I got my arm cut off, it's not like I'd also lose some part of my mind; my mind has no parts. My mind has different *powers*, sure, but when I imagine or conceive or remember or whatever, I'm using my whole entire mind just in different modes. Those aren't *parts I can cut off*, they're just *modes I can exercise or not*.

On the other hand, bodies are divisible; in fact, that's part of what it means to be a body. I don't even know what an indivisible extended thing would *be* like. Point to a body, and I could chop that shit up all kinds of ways.

— **20**

Second, even though the mind and the body are fused together, the mind doesn't get signals from everywhere at once, right? I'll bet it's more like there's a single spot in the brain that the mind is sort of "plugged into," and all the information that goes from body to mind goes through there. It's like a cockpit or a command center with a bunch of levers: each lever triggers a single perception in the mind, and each lever always triggers the exact same perception. So you've got a lever for "my foot tickles" and another one for "fuck I'm thirsty" and so on. That explains those crazy experiments where we make people think their legs are moving by shocking the brain in certain ways, even though their legs are aren't moving at all: it's like we're pulling the levers with electricity instead of the normal way. Information from the body goes to this "command center," pulls on a lever, and *that's* how the mind finds out about the body.

— **21**

So maybe here's how the body works to pull on those levers: if one part moves a second part that's farther away from the head, (like, say, the

cannot likewise be moved in the same way by any one of the parts that lie between those two, although the most remote part does not act at all. As, for example, in the cord A, B, C, D, [which is in tension], if its last part D, be pulled, the first part A, will not be moved in a different way than it would be were one of the intermediate parts B or C to be pulled, and the last part D meanwhile to remain fixed. And in the same way, when I feel pain in the foot, the science of physics teaches me that this sensation is experienced by means of the nerves dispersed over the foot, which, extending like cords from it to the brain, when they are contracted in the foot, contract at the same time the inmost parts of the brain in which they have their origin, and excite in these parts a certain motion appointed by nature to cause in the mind a sensation of pain, as if existing in the foot; but as these nerves must pass through the tibia, the leg, the loins, the back, and neck, in order to reach the brain, it may happen that although their extremities in the foot are not affected, but only certain of their parts that pass through the loins or neck, the same movements, nevertheless, are excited in the brain by this motion as would have been caused there by a hurt received in the foot, and hence the mind will necessarily feel pain in the foot, just as if it had been hurt; and the same is true of all the other perceptions of our senses.

22 —

I remark, finally, that as each of the movements that are made in the part of the brain by which the mind is immediately affected, impresses it with but a single sensation, the most likely supposition in the circumstances is, that this movement causes the mind to experience, among all the sensations which it is capable of impressing upon it; that one which is the best fitted, and generally the most useful for the preservation of the human body when it is in full health. But experi-

knee moves the foot) the second part (the foot) can be moved by something in-between, too (like the ankle, which is between the foot and the knee.) It's like how we use rope tied to the doorknob so we never have to get up from the couch to let people in on game day: I could pull on the end of the rope, and that would pull on the door, which would open the door, right? Right. But I could also make a freshman pull on the middle of the rope, and that would open the door too, even though the other end of the rope is just lying there on the ground next to me, not moving. So when something hurts my foot, it affects the nerves in my foot. Those nerves run like cords all the way up to the brain, where the mind is plugged in, and it pulls on the "AH FUCK MY FOOT" lever. So it's like each nerve is tied to a different lever. When I step on glass or some shit, the nerve gets pulled on, which pulls the "foot pain" lever, which sends the "foot pain" impression to my mind.

But those nerves don't go straight from the foot to the brain; they have to run all the way up my leg and through my back. So if somehow those nerves get pulled on in the middle, like if I hurt my back or something, it still tugs on the "foot pain" lever, and the mind still gets the signal that the foot is hurt. That explains why when I bang my elbow, suddenly my entire fucking forearm feels like it's on fire, even though it's obviously not actually on fire. I've "pulled on" every nerve passing through the elbow, which includes every nerve for my fingers and hand and arm and everything.

— **22**

So here's where I'm at: the mind only gets impressions from the mind-brain interface, not directly from the body, and each lever in that interface can only send one impression. No matter where the nerve that leads to the foot gets stimulated, it pulls on the same lever, which sends the same impression. What impression should it send? I mean, it could be that every time I stub my toe, the lever that makes me feel hungry gets pulled. Why should my toe be tied to a lever that makes me feel pain in my toe instead?

ence shows us that all the perceptions which nature has given us are
of such a kind as I have mentioned; and accordingly, there is nothing
found in them that does not manifest the power and goodness of God.
Thus, for example, when the nerves of the foot are violently or more
than usually shaken, the motion passing through the medulla of the
spine to the innermost parts of the brain affords a sign to the mind on
which it experiences a sensation, viz, of pain, as if it were in the foot,
by which the mind is admonished and excited to do its utmost to remove the cause of it as dangerous and hurtful to the foot. It is true
that God could have so constituted the nature of man as that the same
motion in the brain would have informed the mind of something altogether different: the motion might, for example, have been the occasion on which the mind became conscious of itself, in so far as it is in
the brain, or in so far as it is in some place intermediate between the
foot and the brain, or, finally, the occasion on which it perceived some
other object quite different, whatever that might be; but nothing of all
this would have so well contributed to the preservation of the body as
that which the mind actually feels. In the same way, when we stand in
need of drink, there arises from this want a certain parchedness in the
throat that moves its nerves, and by means of them the internal parts
of the brain; and this movement affects the mind with the sensation of
thirst, because there is nothing on that occasion which is more useful
for us than to be made aware that we have need of drink for the preservation of our health; and so in other instances.

23

Whence it is quite manifest that, notwithstanding the sovereign
goodness of God, the nature of man, in so far as it is composed of
mind and body, cannot but be sometimes fallacious. For, if there is
any cause which excites, not in the foot, but in some one of the parts of

Answer: because it would be fucking stupid if every time I injured my foot, I felt hungry. I would die almost immediately, either from bleeding out of my foot or from cramming down too many peanut butter sandwiches. I think obviously if I have to pick just one impression for every nerve to send to the mind, it should be the one that's most useful to my general survival, right?

And oh, hey, look! The signals we get from the different parts of our body aren't always right, but they're *usually* right; they are, at the very least, the most useful for surviving. Our mind-body interfaces function as well as they possibly could, which means they are also a reflection of the goodness of God.

So sometimes when my hand hurts, it's because I banged my elbow and not my hand. God could have made it so that the nerves in my hand send the impression "I banged the shit out of my elbow at a weird angle," but should the nerves in my hand really send a signal that's correct only like 10% of the time? Shouldn't it send the signal that's usually the right signal, "Oh fuck I hurt my hand?" That one is going to be way better for my general survival, and survival of the body is the entire point of the senses.

So when my throat gets dry, it triggers a nerve that pulls the "dry throat" lever. That lever could send the impression "probably just the dropsy, don't worry about it!" but think of how fast my hangovers would kill me if I never drank water when my throat was dry. That would be fucking stupid. Instead, I get an impression that makes me want to drink water, which is way better for my survival generally, even if it's not perfect in *every* situation.

— **23**

When you consider all that, it's obviously impossible my nature could include body *and* mind without fucking up occasionally. There has to be only one impression each nerve triggers, which means sacrifices have to be made. If the mind is going to get the wrong signal sometimes, it's obviously better to minimize those errors, right?

the nerves that stretch from the foot to the brain, or even in the brain itself, the same movement that is ordinarily created when the foot is ill affected, pain will be felt, as it were, in the foot, and the sense will thus be naturally deceived; for as the same movement in the brain can but impress the mind with the same sensation, and as this sensation is much more frequently excited by a cause which hurts the foot than by one acting in a different quarter, it is reasonable that it should lead the mind to feel pain in the foot rather than in any other part of the body. And if it sometimes happens that the parchedness of the throat does not arise, as is usual, from drink being necessary for the health of the body, but from quite the opposite cause, as is the case with the dropsical, yet it is much better that it should be deceitful in that instance, than if, on the contrary, it were continually fallacious when the body is well-disposed; and the same holds true in other cases.

24

And certainly this consideration is of great service, not only in enabling me to recognize the errors to which my nature is liable, but likewise in rendering it more easy to avoid or correct them: for, knowing that all my senses more usually indicate to me what is true than what is false, in matters relating to the advantage of the body, and being able almost always to make use of more than a single sense in examining the same object, and besides this, being able to use my memory in connecting present with past knowledge, and my understanding which has already discovered all the causes of my errors, I ought no longer to fear that falsity may be met with in what is daily presented to me by the senses. And I ought to reject all the doubts of those bygone days, as hyperbolical and ridiculous, especially the general uncertainty respecting sleep, which I could not distinguish from the waking state: for I now find a very marked difference between the two states, in respect that our memory can never connect our dreams with each other and with the course of life, in the way it is in the habit of doing

HOW DOES OUR HERO'S EXPLANATION OF THE MIND/BODY RELATIONSHIP
HELP HIM ACCOMPLISH THE GOAL OF THIS MEDITATION?

_____

_____

_____

_____

_____

_____

_____

_____

_____

_____

_____

_____

_____

— **24**

Here's the other thing! Now that I've been over all this shit, it'll be really easy for me to avoid those avoidable errors in my nature, because I can double check using multiple senses. "Oh, my hand hurts, but I just hit my elbow? Maybe that thing with the nerves that happens sometimes is happening again, let me check—yup, my hand appears to be totally fine. See, wasn't that easy to double-check like an adult instead of fucking panicking?" I have nothing to be afraid of: my senses get things right as often as they can, and even in the rare cases they do fuck up, I have other resources to back me up and double-check.

Honestly, in hindsight, all my doubts and worries seem kind of fucking silly. I mean, "How do I know I'm not sleeping?" Easy, stupid: in dreams, the memory is never drawing connections to other dreams. When I'm awake, my memory is constantly connecting dreams to each other and to my life. So, there's an easy way to tell if I'm dreaming or not: can I remember other dreams? If not, I'm dreaming. Oh, plus, in real life, shit never appears out of absolutely nowhere. When it appears out of

with events that occur when we are awake. And, in truth, if some one, when I am awake, appeared to me all of a sudden and as suddenly disappeared, as do the images I see in sleep, so that I could not observe either whence he came or whither he went, I should not without reason esteem it either a specter or phantom formed in my brain, rather than a real man. But when I perceive objects with regard to which I can distinctly determine both the place whence they come, and that in which they are, and the time at which they appear to me, and when, without interruption, I can connect the perception I have of them with the whole of the other parts of my life, I am perfectly sure that what I thus perceive occurs while I am awake and not during sleep. And I ought not in the least degree to doubt of the truth of these presentations, if, after having called together all my senses, my memory, and my understanding for the purpose of examining them, no deliverance is given by any one of these faculties which is repugnant to that of any other: for since God is no deceiver, it necessarily follows that I am not herein deceived. But because the necessities of action frequently oblige us to come to a determination before we have had leisure for so careful an examination, it must be confessed that the life of man is frequently obnoxious to error with respect to individual objects; and we must, in conclusion, ac. knowledge the weakness of our nature.

nowhere in dreams, I'm like, "Oh." But in real life, I can trace the origin of things and connect my impressions to other moments in my life, to other memories I have. My senses, my memory, and my understanding all come together to help me decide whether or not I'm dreaming, and they all agree: not dreaming. At this point, I have no reason to doubt that I'm awake, since all of those faculties are given to me by a God who is not a fucking liar.

It was really nice to be careful for the past week or so and really think things through, but scared and overthoughtful is no way to go through life. Sometimes, we have to make the best of what we know, which means sometimes getting it wrong. The good news is, God has given us tools to correct ourselves, so we don't have to be afraid, even of the mistakes we make. So here's the plan: I'mma admit my faults and acknowledge the weakness in my nature, and then…

I'mma get real fucked up.

YOU MADE IT! WHAT DOES OUR HERO THINK HE ACCOMPLISHED OVER THE LAST SIX DAYS?

_____

_____

_____

_____

ABOUT THE AUTHOR

· · ·

Tommy Maranges studied philosophy at Notre Dame, where he didn't really go to football games, but he did lead the standup club. He lives in Chicago, Illinois.

A NOTE ON THE TYPE

. . .

Descartes' Meditations, Bro is set primarily in three typefaces. The primary text and reference text are set in Freight Sans and Freight Text, respectively, both of which were designed by Joshua Darden of The Darden Studio. Additional information, page numbers, and headings are set in Replica, which was designed by Norm, a design firm comprising Dimitri Bruni and Manuel Krebs.

Printed and bound by Sheridan Books, Chelsea, Michigan.
Designed by Brandon Keelean.